Criminal Justice
Recent Scholarship

Edited by
Marilyn McShane and Frank P. Williams III

A Series from LFB Scholarly

Gangs and Immigrant Youth

Kyung-Seok Choo

LFB Scholarly Publishing LLC
New York 2007

Library of Congress Cataloging-in-Publication Data

Choo, Kyung-Seok, 1969-
  Gangs and immigrant youth / Kyung-Seok Choo.
    p. cm. -- (Criminal justice : recent scholarship)
  Includes bibliographical references and index.
  ISBN-10: 1-59332-148-1 (alk. paper)
  ISBN-13: 978-1-59332-148-2 (alk. paper)
  1. Gangs--United States. 2. Juvenile delinquents--United States. 3.
Korean Americans. 4. Korean Americans--Social conditions. 5.
Juvenile delinquency--United States. 6. Violence--United States. I.
Title.
  HV6439.U5C48 2007
  364.106'6089957073--dc22

2006029527

ISBN-10 1593321481
ISBN-13 9781593321482

Printed on acid-free 250-year-life paper.

Manufactured in the United States of America.

To my daughters Beitrice and Iris

Table of Contents

List of Tables

List of Figures

Acknowledgments

The completion of this book would not have been possible without the support of my family who has provided a never-ending source of strength, love and encouragement for me, not only during this project but also throughout my entire life. All my accomplishments are a direct result of the love and support provided by my family, you all know who you are.

I have been fortunate to have wonderful professors and staffs who supported and encouraged my academic work: Freda Adler, Ko-lin Chin, Ronald V. Clarke, Marcus Felson, James O. Finckenauer, Clayton A. Hartjen, Leslie W. Kennedy, Edith Laurencin, Michael G. Maxfield, Phyllis Schultze, Mercer L. Sullivan, Bonita M. Veysey at School of Criminal Justice, Rutgers University. Robert Kelly at City University of New York. Throughout my interaction with each of them, I experienced intellectual growth and solid scholarship. Especially, Dr. Ko-lin Chin has provided professional and personal guidance, and a solid foundation from which to begin, what I hope to be, a wonderful academic career. Dr. Mercer L. Sullivan trained me as an ethnographic researcher to initiate this project. His scholarly advice and helpful criticism have bestowed upon me the confidence to do so. I am also very grateful to the late Professor Gerhard O.W. Mueller of Rutgers University for his encouragement and guidance to international and comparative aspect of criminology.

In addition, I would like to express my gratitude to the faculties, administrators, and staffs at Utica College for providing crucial support in numerous ways: President Todd S. Hutton, Vice President for Academic Affairs Judith A. Kirkpatrick, Dean of Social Sciences and Management John H. Johnsen, Execute Director Bruce R. McBride and Director George Curtis at Center for Economic Crime and Justice Studies. And to staffs at Social Science Division: Ms. Sue Cox, Karen Kateta, and Louis Phelps. I also like to thank Mary Anne Hutchinson who reviewed every word of this book, and enhanced its clarity and accuracy.

I am also indebted to those who share their professional experience with Korean youth groups in Korean communities. They are detectives Jae-Il Shim, Mark Bendall, Dale Loyer and social workers Sang-Sook (Grace) Lee and Chung Park. Finally, my deepest appreciation goes to Korean youths who participated in this research.

CHAPTER 1

Introduction

Many efforts have been made to determine the origin of youth gang problems in the United States. From Thrasher's 1927 book, *The Gang: A Study of One Thousand Three Hundred Thirteen Gangs in Chicago*, published in 1927, to contemporary research, a wealth of material is now available, covering a broad range of activities. Nevertheless, our understanding of gang issues remains unclear due to the dynamic and changing nature of gangs (Short, 1996). The diversity of gangs today, when compared to those in the past, has been well documented. Recent research has identified several important aspects of that diversity. The number of cities with gang problems, for instance, has sharply increased since the 1980s (Miller, 2001; National Youth Gang Center, 2000). The 2002-2003 National Youth Gang Survey also indicates the increased gang problems remain stable and predominantly concentrated in larger cities (Egley, 2005). The average age of youth gang members today tends to be older than in the past, due to a lack of legitimate jobs for youths (Hagedorn, 1998; Moore, 1991; Egley & Arjunan, 2002). An increase in lethal violence has also been identified a result of the widespread availability of weapons (Blumstein, 2002; Sanders, 1994; Thornberry, Krohn, Lizotte, Smith & Tobin, 2003). Change across gender lines has also been observed. Although male gang members still outnumber females by a wide margin, the increase in female involvement in gang activity is undeniable (Campbell, 1990; Chesney,

1

Lind, Sheldon, & Joe, 1996; Eghigian and Kirby, 2006; Miller, 2001; Moore, 1991). Moreover, new forms of gangs have also emerged. Chin (1990, 1996), English (1995), and Vigil and Yun (1990) found Asian gangs to be quite distinct in terms of their patterns of gang behaviors.

In this book, I explore this last point in more detail by examining group delinquency among young Korean people in the United States. The context of this study is necessarily narrow, in that its primary focus is a comparison of two distinct youth groups, a Korean affiliated Chinese youth gang and a Korean delinquent group. The terms "youth gang" and "delinquent group" are clarified later. The youth gang is located in a New York City-based Korean community that is surrounded by a large Chinese community, while the delinquent group is in a Korean community in New Jersey where no other distinct ethnic group coexists. The two groups have evolved through different processes and under different community circumstances. Even though they are both law-violating groups, they manifest differing patterns of delinquent activities, which require different approaches to their problems. In a sense, this research can be viewed as a case study of an immigrant ethnic group in specific and separate areas of the United States.

Four initiatives are used in conducting this study and are reflected throughout this book. In order, these initiatives:

1. Provide substantial evidence of group delinquency in the Korean community as an emerging social problem.
2. Examine the demographic, socioeconomic, and cultural characteristics of the Korean immigrant community that shape the unique lifestyle of Korean-American immigrants in correlation to their youth and group delinquency problem.
3. Understand the phenomenon of "gangs and immigrant youth," using historical analyses of youth gangs in the immigrant community.
4. Integrate these initiatives together to explain by detailed comparison the emergence, development, persistence and change of two distinctive groups, a youth gang and a delinquent group in Korean communities.

KOREAN YOUTH GANG AS AN EMERGING SOCIAL PROBLEM

The image Korean immigrants once held as a "model minority" because of their hard-work ethic and their children's success in schoolwork has been damaged recently by alarming news stories about youth gang problems. In recent years, major U.S. newspapers have repeatedly published reports about the viciousness and cruelty of Korean gangs. For example, an article from the *New York Daily News* reported on a court case in which two Korean youth gang members lured a cabbie to his death, solely for the purpose of buying beer and trying to impress future gang members (Fenner, 2001). Three months later, the same source again reported a shocking story about four members of a Flushing, Queens-based Korean gang that forced their victim to eat dog food, and then burned his tongue with a cigarette. They were arrested by the FBI-NYPD Asian Organized Crime squad (Claffey, 2001). The *New York Times* also reported an extortion case in which a Korean businessman was arrested for threatening to send Korean gang members to disrupt a nightclub business in the Korean community (Kershaw, 2001). According to *U.S. Federal News* (2006), the U.S. Department of Homeland Security's Immigration and Customs Enforcement announced that two New York City Police Officers along with two gang members were arrested on bribery charges relating to the protection of a brothel located in Flushing, Queens. The news also reported agents seized approximately $800,000 in cash, believed to be the proceeds of the brothel.

Headline news stories about gang related crimes and the attendant fear and concern in Korean communities continue to fill the airwaves and are plastered on the front pages of Korean ethnic newspapers as well. Over the past five years from 2000 to 2005, numerous articles from *Joong-Ang Daily News* and *Han-Kook Daily News* reported Korean gang related robberies, burglaries, homicides, assaults, and extortion. In these reports, Korean Power was the most frequently cited gang name in the New York Korean community and in Los Angeles it was the Korean Killers. Interestingly, some articles also indicated that some Korean gang factions or cliques are formed within Chinese gangs, using names like Korean Fuk Ching, Korean Flying Dragons, Mo Ming Pai, and Four Seas.

A 1997 report from the New York Korean Youth Center located in Flushing also indicates the seriousness of Korean youth gang-related problems in New York. The report shows that about 33% (383 out of 774) of the adolescents served by the center are in some way involved in gang-related activities. Data on gang-related problems includes runaways, drugs, and other activities. Hotline counselor Sang-Sook Lee (personal interview, October 1998) explains that almost every adolescent runaway she counseled was likely to be a participant in gang activities, and some were involved in drug distribution such as selling marijuana or Ecstasy to their friends. She also maintained that more than 80% of the female cases were involved in gang problems. Although many females were not regarded as gang members per se, they did, however, frequently associate with and hang out with male gang members. This statement supports Chin's research on Chinatown gangs in New York (1996), indicating that many Korean girls do tend to hang around with Chinese gang members.

The Korean gang problem elicits negative responses from law enforcement agencies. At one point, the Los Angeles police chief claimed that there was a major Korean "godfather" figure who employed 400 thugs. Los Angeles police arrested some gang members in this instance, despite the fact that the godfather figure was not identified (Waters, 1999). According to a Korean detective, Jae I. Shim (personal interview, August 1998), responsible for monitoring Korean gang activity in Flushing's 109th Precinct, Korean youth gangs continue to generate massive problems for Korean families and for the Korean community as a whole in New York. He expressed concern over the exposure of Korean American adolescents to Korean gang-related soap operas and movies [1]. This kind of entertainment is generally crude and seldom truly represents reality; it can nevertheless have a very negative effect on the behavior of Korean American youth. This is especially so when famous actors play law enforcement officers, and use violence in the name of justice.

Overall, the furor over the serious gang problem is widespread. The community response has been to educate and warn parents about their children's potential gang association, to identify possible causes, and to point fingers occasionally at each other (personal observation in community meetings, June 1998; August 1999; July 2000; August

---

[1] There are many Korean video shops in the Korean community. Koreans can rent almost all popular TV series and movies just a couple of days after release in Korea.

2001). Thus far, however, we have not heard from law-violating Korean groups themselves. Systematic and academic research on Korean American group delinquency is warranted.

THE KOREAN COMMUNITY: UNIQUE LIFE-STYLES OF KOREAN IMMIGRANTS

Understanding Korean American group delinquency necessarily requires a familiarity with relevant social, cultural, economic and political issues that shape the Korean community environment. Only then can the dynamics of formation and development of law-violating youth groups be fully understood. Klein (1995) and Thrasher (1927) have argued that there is not likely to be one characteristic gang situation and that "no two gangs are just alike." Not only do the characteristics of gangs differ from community to community, but they also differ within the community itself as they emerge and develop. These perspectives and concepts will be utilized to focus and analyze the ethnographic data of Korean American youth experiences and to stimulate further questions and discussions intersecting relationships along the immigration process, the gangs, the delinquent groups, and the community.

Since Korean immigration into the United States began in 1902, Korean immigrants have developed unique lifestyles through their various personal and collective experiences. This has often led to adverse social consequences in urban centers of the United States. One common method used to overcome the various disadvantages imposed on them is the development and maintenance of a high level of ethnic attachment or ethnicity, which consists of a unique bond based on a shared culture among members that causes them to consider themselves a group distinguishable from others. These immigrants could never entirely dispel the influence of their former life in Korea. It is fair to say that Korean immigrants hold their ethnicity in higher regard than any other Asian American group (Min, 1995; 2006). The most conspicuous and uniform features that sets Korean Americans off from their fellow Americans is that they speak Korean at home, eat Korean food daily, and practice their traditional customs on a regular basis. Korean Americans prefer Korean language media and are the most likely segment of Asian Americans to read one or more in-language newspapers on a daily basis (Hurh, 1998).

Other ethnic media, including Korean Radio and TV programs, also play a role in maintaining their high level of ethnic attachment. However, most Korean children, particularly those born in this country, cannot speak Korean fluently. It is not unusual that parents speak Korean and children speak English in many of these families (Lee, 2004; Park, 1995). When complex issues are discussed between parents and children, subtleties of thought and emotion are often missed and miscommunication often results. In addition, children of Korean immigrants dress and act like other American youths. They are very much Americanized. They like listening to rap music, and show a high level of interest in following the current fashions and fads. They also enjoy Internet-related activities such as chat rooms and game playing, instead of relaxing with traditional Korean music and cultural activities. They are now moving in the direction of a more complete assimilation with the American mainstream youth culture. Value conflicts, combined with language barriers, often lead to an unbridgeable distance between Korean parents and their children (Min, 1995).

The following statements on economic patterns from the 2000 Census, regarding Korean Americans, show that the children of Korean immigrants are more vulnerable than other groups to peer-group pressure and as a result are more likely to form delinquent groups and gangs. No major ethnic group in the United States exceeded Korean Americans in terms of the percentage who are self-employed (19.9%). A remarkably high proportion (31%) of Korean Americans work in retail. The high concentration of small businesses owned by Korean immigrants is another response of that community as a group to overcome certain disadvantages in the American labor market. These include and are due to the language barrier, and cultural unfamiliarity, as well as educational credentials and occupational skills that are not easily transferable from their native country to the United States (Hurh, 1998). Since many Korean small businesses are open twenty-four hours a day, or well past midnight, and utilize unpaid support by family members (mostly spouses), the small business activities among Korean Americans often lead to family and youth problems in the community at large. With a lack of parental control or supervision after school and during school breaks, Korean children are likely to spend their spare time together on the street, in Internet cafés, or at billiard clubs. As Warr (1993) found, parents who spend more time with their offspring may reduce the likelihood of their children associating with delinquent peers. The importance of supervising spare time for children is evident in the following quotation from an ethnographic study of American youth undertaken in the early decades of the twentieth century:

> The most important agency in directing the spare time activities of the boy is the family. In the under privileged classes, family life in a large number of cases fails to provide for or control the leisure-time behavior of the adolescent.... The boy with time on his hands, especially in a crowded or slum environment is almost predestined to the life of the gang, which is simply a substitute, although a most satisfactory one from the boy's point of view, for activities and controls not otherwise provided. (Thrasher, 1927, p. 65)

Once children of Korean descent have tasted the thrilling street life where American youth culture and delinquent group activities already exist, it appears that many gradually spend less and less of their time in school and work. More time is spent with other unsupervised peers, who generally have the same interests as well as similar generational, cultural, and value conflicts encountered in the adjustment process to the larger social milieu. It is important to note that young Koreans are influenced not only by American youth culture, but also by other ethnic delinquent subcultures in their neighborhood. Delinquent groups, for example, exist in the Korean communities in both New York and New Jersey. But youth gangs, affiliated with Chinese gangs or having a similar structure and criminal activities as Chinese gangs, have been seen only in a New York Korean community that was surrounded by a Chinese community. This group difference will be fully elaborated in chapter 6 and 7.

The passion for education and high academic achievement also plays an important role in Korean American life. The historical legacy of attaining social mobility through education - especially political and financial success - is deeply rooted in the Korean tradition and consciousness (Savana & Shaw, 1990). Whether in Korea or in America, Korean parents' primary concern is to provide their children with the best education possible. Many Korean parents send their children to private institutions after school to prepare for admission to prestigious colleges and universities. In 2000, ninety-four private institutions gave various courses, including English and math lessons, to Korean American students in Flushing, New York, alone. A large number of Korean students do exceed average academic performance; a significant proportion of them, however, do not meet their parents' educational expectations (Min, 1995). As Sullivan (1989) indicated, the patterns of either school involvement, or leaving school and the lack of education could play a crucial role in future options for young people. However, as will be seen later, too much emphasis on education may lead to psychological stress among Korean American youth, who justify their regular grouping in private educational institutions without genuine interests in education. Furthermore, those who fail to be academically competitive may lose interest in school and subsequently engage in delinquency and gang activities (Yu, 1987).

There is a popular saying among Korean Americans: "When two Japanese meet, they set up a business; when two Chinese meet, they open a Chinese restaurant; and when two Koreans meet, they establish a church." (Hurh, 1998) The churches in Korean communities have provided not only spiritual fellowship, but also ethnic camaraderie, cultural identity, and social services. The community role of the Korean church has led to a phenomenal increase in their actual number. Some reports indicate that there are over 2,800 Korean churches in the United States (Hurh, 1998; Kim, 1997). Compared with other Korean ethnic associations, the church is by far the most popular and important institution for the individual, regardless of gender, age, economic status, or whether a newcomer or settled person in the US. Interestingly, I found that most community programs for Korean youth and gang prevention were initiated through these religious institutions. Lee (1998), however, found that many such programs have a difficult time reaching out to adolescents who need help. Many parents feel shame or experience a loss of face if they believe that others know about their children's involvement in gang-related activities. For that reason, they do not seek help through professional counselors or community organizations. And, for those who do, many of their young people find these programs insipid and unsatisfying.

Korean Americans seem to possess a number of distinct characteristics that differentiate their social and cultural situation from that of other ethnic groups. Whether these characteristics are likely to continue, or whether they are an outcome of a relatively short immigration history remains to be seen. Nonetheless, the characteristics that distinguish Korean immigrants from other ethnic immigrants with a similar cultural background are their distinctive educational goals, inclination toward small retail business operations, and a high level of religious participation. These factors have contributed to their different forms of social structure and activity in their ethnic enclaves of the United States.

At the same time, children of Korean immigrants experience the social web of interaction through the immigration process characterized by such elements as the generational gap, culture and value conflicts, exposure to mainstream American youth culture, and lack of supervision and programs offered by the recognized social agencies within the ethnic community. As youths, they are incapable of analyzing the complex forces operating within the community that create this environment and stimulate nonconformity and rebellious behavior. Through these and other aspects of the Korean immigrant situation, nontraditional norms and values are instilled, educational goals and social capital disregarded, and future opportunities lost for young members of this community.

It would be presumptuous to take it for granted that all Korean youths in this situation will form a gang or engage in gang related activities. But, as will be seen later, many young Korean-Americans are likely to become involved in law-violating youth groups or related issues.

GANGS AND IMMIGRANT YOUTH

The perceived link between immigration and crime continues to fuel national debates (See Butcher & Piehl, 1998; Horowitz, 2001), partly due to the data ambiguity issue (McCord, 1995; Tonry, 1997) and partly due to the complexity and diversity of the phenomena of delinquency and crime within the social and political structure. The topic "immigrant youth gang" lost its appeal when European immigrant youth gangs gradually disappeared through assimilation and acculturation. Sutherland and Cressey (1974) in the ninth edition of their classic text *Criminology* described the relationship between immigration and crime as no longer an important focus of American sociology.

As scientific inquiry changes, most gang researchers have shifted their focus to ethnic minorities in major cities. The concentration of ethnic minorities in urban centers began after World War II and facilitated the migration of African Americans from the rural south into the nation's major cities. Large numbers of Hispanic immigrants came to major cities in the U.S. to find jobs and, in the process, helped to fill them. Unlike youth gangs of European immigrants, black and Hispanic gangs faced problems dealing with racial conflict or class stratification, as opposed to problems dealing with immigration and social integration. It may be due to the fact that black gangs did not go through the international immigration process, while Hispanic gangs continue to exist more than three generations beyond the assimilation and acculturation period. As a result, "gangs" simply came to mean "black" or "Hispanic" problems, completely ignoring the immigration impact until the emergence of new Asian gangs challenged the ethnic pattern of gangs.

This study seeks to establish three general research findings in the study of the gang or group delinquency problem and immigrant youth. First, group delinquency occurs more often than not as a youth phenomena (Bursik & Grasmick, 1993; Erickson & Jensen, 1977; Reiss, 1988; Shaw & McKay, 1942; Short & Strodtbeck, 1965; Zimring, 1981). Second, group delinquency is likely to occur among immigrant youth undergoing a cross-generational and acculturation process, which gravitates forward peer group socialization (Thrasher, 1927; Vigil, 2003; Waters, 1999; Whyte, 1943). Third, group delinquency, particularly gang problems, has clearly emerged in almost all immigrant enclaves in the urban landscape of America (Asbury, 1927; Chin, 1996; Jankowski, 1991; Moore, 1991; Padilla, 1992; Shaw & McKay, 1942; Vigil, 1990). Through U.S. history, it has often been noted that gang problems coincide with an increase in immigration. Historical analysis supports this observation.

As early as the 18th century, gangs were identified in the streets of New York City (Sante, 1991). By the time Irish immigrants settled in the Five Points District of Manhattan, about 1820, some of these early youth gangs had hundreds of members (Haskins, 1974). According to Asbury (1927), Irish youth gangs were said to have precipitated the New York City Civil War draft riots. It has been estimated that by 1855, at least 30,000 men in New York City were associated with gangs (Asbury, 1927).

In the late 19th and early 20th centuries, the United States experienced an influx of European immigrants. At the same time, children of various ethnic groups from eastern and southern Europe (Poland, Italy, Germany, Russia) were often involved in youth gangs in the large cities of the Northeast region. In the 1940s when Mexican immigrants appeared in California and the southwest, Mexican youth gangs were identified in these immigrant communities (Moore, 1991). The Mexican immigrant gang has been known as a long lasting, rather than transitory, phenomenon, much beyond the expected assimilation and acculturation time period. This may be due to a unique situation of continuous migration from Mexico, which produces new cycles of marginality where established members continually recruit newer arrivals (Vigil, 1988). Moore, Vigil and Garcia (1983) also note that although the barrios where the gangs persist are areas of first settlement for immigrants; the population turnover is very high due to a continuous immigrant flow. Thus, immigration processes play an important role in understanding the emergence and longevity of these gangs. It was not until the passage of the 1965 Immigration Act that Asian immigrants groups rapidly appeared on the American scene. Like earlier immigrants, they are concentrated in major U.S. cities. Not surprisingly, the problem of Asian youth gangs emerged and became of vital concern in the early 1970s (Chin, 1996; English, 1995; Vigil &Yun, 1990). Likewise, Korean youth gang problems were first identified in the Los Angeles Korean community in the late 1970s and in the New York Korean community in the early 1980s (Min, 1995). This historical pattern of gang emergence may be a critical factor in explaining the current wave of new ethnic gangs in inner city areas.

From an historical perspective, Thrasher's observation (1927) seems to be still valid to the extent that a gang is a natural response of immigrant youth to a disorganized marginal immigrant community. The idea of the "disorganized community" was, however, challenged by Whyte (1943), who found youth gangs in an Italian immigrant community known as Cornerville, which was inhabited almost exclusively by Italians of lower socioeconomic status, to be very well structured and organized. Regardless of the degree of community stability, it is hard to deny that there have been regular and repeated occurrences of group delinquency and/or gang activity in urban immigrant communities. As Waters (1999) concludes in his comparative ethnic analysis of crime and immigrant youth, the formation of youth gangs is a product of the process of migration. In a sense, the black gang problem in major U.S. cities can be explained by the migrant group process, in that a large number of African Americans migrated from the rural south to northern U.S. cities after World War II. According to Spergel (1995), restrictive immigration during the late 1920s and 1930s slowed the arrival of low-cost labor from Europe. African Americans from the rural south, along with Mexican immigrants were pulled in to serve as a new source of cheap labor.

Furthermore, it was the degree of community stability that produced a disparate number of distinguishing characteristics, and stability of the resultant gangs (Klein, 1995). Community stability also stimulates specific forms and patterns of group delinquency within a given immigrant group as well as between immigrant groups. A study of these trends provides the foundation for this research, which is aimed at stressing the importance of understanding different peer group aspects and relationships in cases of adolescent delinquency, and youth gang versus delinquent youth, in the Korean American immigrant community.

YOUTH GANGS AND DELINQUENT GROUPS

Our understanding of the nature and extent of social problems and our responses to them depends heavily on how they are defined. The term gang is always nebulous: it can easily mislead laypeople and even academic scholars. A gang is too complex an entity to judge its nature based on merely a few indicators. This becomes obvious when the variety of meanings gangs have taken on for researchers, practitioners, and the young people who are members of youth groups themselves, are considered. For these reasons, the lines between gangs and other delinquent groups are often blurred. Nonetheless, research through the years shows that most juvenile delinquency is conducted by a small companionship group, consisting of two or three boys, who do not constitute true gangs (Howell & Egley, 2005; Miller, 1982; Reiss, 1988; Short & Strodtbeck, 1965; Shaw & McKay, 1942; Warr, 1996). These small and informal groups differ from youth gangs in numerous ways. They are sometimes treated as embryonic gangs, known as cliques, which form themselves within a gang (Thrasher, 1927), but have sometimes emerged independently and operate under quite different group processes and structures (Klein, 1971). Most importantly, they engage in delinquent activities that are different from those of the large social aggregates identified as gangs (Battin-Pearson, Thornberry, Hawkins, & Krohn, 1998; Hakkert, 1998; Thornberry, Krohn, Lizotte, Smith, & Tobin. 2003).

Since there is no consensus on the definition of gang, or even a clear distinction from other delinquent groups, the first task must be to clearly set forth the distinguishing differences between gangs and delinquent groups. The inquiry begins with how previous researchers differentiate them. Some distinguish gangs from delinquent groups explicitly while others, like Reiss (1988), develop alternative phrases such as "co-offending" in order to avoid conceptual ambiguities. Still others use the term "delinquent peers" (Matsueda & Anderson, 1998; Warr, 1993), without clarifying the difference between gang and youth groups (But also see Warr, 1996 for distinction between gang and delinquent group).

A number of researchers (Curry & Spergel, 1993; Miller, 1982; Oehme, 1997; Sullivan, 2000) identify the differences in characteristics between gang and other law-violating youth groups. They consider gangs only one of several deviant peer groups in inner city environments. Curry and Spergel (1993) differentiate them by group behavioral patterns, specifically asserting that group delinquency is law-violating behavior committed by juveniles in relatively ephemeral small groups. In comparison, gang activity is defined as law-violating behavior committed by either juveniles or adults in/or related to groups that are complexly organized, sometimes cohesive, and sometimes with established leadership roles and rules. From their perspective, the concepts of the delinquent group and the youth gang are not mutually exclusive, but rather represent distinct configurations of related social phenomena. Miller (1982) also conceptualizes gang and law-violating youth groups separately. Both groups are engaged in illegal activities. However, organization, structure, and turf are the main characteristics of gangs, while moral support and cooperation in a less formal and more flexible setting are attributes of other delinquent groups. Others, like Sullivan (2000), identify three distinct groups: action-sets, cliques, and gangs. He distinguishes them according to their formalization and persistence over time. An action-set is an aggregation of individuals cooperating together in a coordinated line of activity. Action-sets resemble the concept of co-offenders by Reiss (1988), because they can easily disappear after completion of their coordinated activity. Sullivan's definition of a clique is an aggregation of individuals with some form of diffuse and enduring bond of solidarity that partakes in common activities on a regular basis. The difference between a clique and a gang is that a gang requires explicit criteria, such as a name, for membership recognized by themselves and others. With different classifications of groups, these scholars suggest that gangs and delinquent groups represent two quite distinct phenomena, each requiring different intervention and prevention strategies.

The Korean-American detective Shim (personal interview, August 1998) describes these two distinct peer aspects of delinquency within the Korean community. According to him, some youth gangs, like the Korean Ghost Shadows and Korean Power, are organized and maintain loose ties with adult organizations. But, for the most part, they are simply a large group of friends who hang out together and get into fistfights with other gangs. Moreover, many delinquent groups in Korean communities are confusedly identified with gangs because they may adopt a few gang characteristics, such as a designated turf, and a distinctive dress, with colors. Delinquent groups have existed in almost all communities as the most prevalent form of all deviant youth groups, before dramatic gang proliferation in recent years was reported across U.S. cities. They are in fact ephemeral, engage in relatively minor delinquent acts and have little if any actual or ongoing contact with youth gangs. Whether recent reports of increased gang problems in cities represent reality or moral panic, our understanding of the phenomenon can be limited if no clarification is made between these two groups (Egley, 2005; Klein, 1995; Maxson, 1998; Miller, 2001; National Youth Gang Center, 1997, 1998, 1999, 2000). Thus, the youth gang and the delinquent group must be carefully examined in order to measure the actual scope of the problem that each group poses to the community at large and to the social development of its members.

PURPOSE AND RESEARCH QUESTIONS OF THE STUDY

The purpose of this study is to explore not only the causation and formation of Korean youth gangs and delinquent groups, but also their comparative development and changes. Exploring the perspectives of the two different groups in two different communities will help us to understand the variations between these groups, as well as individual group member variations. In order to accomplish this, the study will also examine the ecological context, the structure of the gang as well as their dynamics—local context, family, school, age, size, sub groupings, leadership, interaction with Chinese gang members, association with adult criminal groups, the role of Korean females, types of associated activities--such as drugs and violence, and the places where their illegal activities occur.

The methods used for this study are face-to-face interviews and field observation. Ecological factors such as family, school, and local context are all measured. Questions are asked to measure kinship factors such as stability and socialization in the family, as well as educational indicators like truancy and dropout, to identify the causation of Korean youths' gang involvement. The physical characteristics of the community setting are observed to understand how environmental factors affect their behavior. Ad hoc community meetings are also used to measure community awareness and response to the youth gang problem. Likewise, structural factors that contribute to their group dynamics are obtained through the individual member's oral history data and field observations.

Through these methods, the following research questions are addressed. The main question driving this study is simple: what is the precise nature of the two different law-violating Korean youth groups that are being examined. Determining what is at stake in such a question naturally leads to further questions. For example, why is there a different mode of law-violating youth groups found in Korean communities? Since youth gangs are only reported in a New York Korean community, the dimensions of local Korean community structure are examined to answer the question. How do communities differ in terms of age, sex, school performance, family and other social variables? Assessing these variables provided correlates, or conditions, that accompany the formation of law-violating youth groups. What determines the relative stability or instability of these youth groups? Why are the delinquent groups ephemeral compared to youth gangs, if they actually are? What types of activities and structure constitute Korean youth gangs? Do these activities have certain patterns such as time and place? Are there any intragroup or intergroup conflicts? Why do some Korean youths affiliate with Chinese gangs? What is the Korean community response and level of awareness to its youth problems? These questions will be addressed on the basis of data obtained by interviews, participant observation and local official data.

IMPORTANCE OF THE RESEARCH

Exploring group delinquency and gang-related problems in the Korean community is important for several reasons. Unlike the Chinese and Vietnamese youth gangs, or delinquent groups where law enforcement authorities maintained some record of their past and current activities, there is a dearth of studies concerning Korean American gangs and group delinquency in the United States. This can be attributed, in large part, to a perception that the phenomenon is statistically rare. The prevailing perception is not unreasonable. Viewed from a distance, outside the ethnic community, Korean children might give the impression of being a hard-working academic success story, which because of their visibility and the distance from their observers gives them the appearance of being role models among youth. The same phenomenon viewed from the inside presents a different picture entirely. What we know about Korean law-violating youth groups mainly comes from newspaper articles and one or two pages of brief description under the Asian gang section in major gang related books. As a result of this void in research, very little is known about actual youth gang and group criminal patterns in Korean communities, and the structural determinants that contribute to their formation and perpetuation.

From a public health perspective, fear of the dangers posed by gang members and group delinquency in general may disturb the social, educational, and psychological development of the young generation of Korean Americans. One of the most important motivations of Korean immigrants who come to the United States is to provide a better education for their children and to improve their living conditions (Hurh, 1998). These parents become concerned about safety or gang activity with regard to their children. Moreover, these families may find it difficult to adjust to their new environment and this may weaken the ability of the community to solve gang problems.

From a criminal justice perspective, as the population of various ethnic groups increases in the United States, criminal justice authorities must adopt an ever increasing number of strategies to deal effectively with the wide range of ethnic minorities within the community. In order to cope with gang and delinquent groups and their illegal and violent activities, criminal justice authorities need to understand the Korean culture and community dynamics. Identifying predictors of gang association can also help with these issues.

Should the study demonstrate that there are a small but significant number of Korean youths who are involved in gang activities and that this ethnic minority has been neglected by the criminal justice system, it would then be incumbent on criminal justice authorities and criminologists to develop a response to group delinquency among Korean youth. This study provides insight into the Korean American society in the northeastern region of the USA where little academic research on Korean American youth gangs has to this point been conducted. By familiarizing ourselves with the problems experienced by Korean youth who are at risk, or of gang members themselves, we can develop strategies to deal with them.

CHAPTER 2
Review of the Literature

This chapter is intended to provide background information on hypotheses about group delinquency problems and their framework within the Korean American immigrant community. The following four areas are reviewed: diversity of law-violating youth groups, immigration and theories of gangs, historical context of Korean immigration, and the experience of the children of Korean immigrants. Group offending committed by Korean immigrant youth gangs and delinquent groups cannot be understood, nor can its impact be evaluated, without first understanding the structural and behavioral diversities within them. For that reason, the review begins with the existing body of knowledge on the diversity of law-violating youth groups. The term "law-violating youth groups" is here used to reflect both youth gang and delinquent groups. Next, gang theories are reformulated in the context of the immigration phenomenon in order to understand the relationship between immigration and the gang process. A brief history of Korean immigration follows. The Korean immigration history is, in itself, worthy of study in order to uncover the factors and conditions in which Korean immigrants settle and became acculturated. One of the first lessons from this immigration history will focus on the experiences and circumstances in which young Koreans are socialized and which make them react and respond to gang pressures. The experience of Korean immigrant youth will be reviewed within the process of identity adaptation. These themes are both directly and indirectly related to Korean American gang/group delinquency.

THE DIVERSITY OF THE LAW-VIOLATING YOUTH GROUP

This section reviews the diversity of law-violating youth groups, focusing on structural and behavioral dimensions linked to research questions in the study. Since the diverse nature of these groups requires different strategies, identifying these characteristics can lead to a more appropriate response toward these groups.

Structural Characteristics: Size, Age, Subgroups, and Leadership

Understanding the organizational structure of the gang and other delinquent groups plays an important role in understanding the function of the groups themselves. The components of the group structure have indispensable functions for each other. Demographic variables such as age, subgroup, size, and leadership role are all components of the group structure on varying levels of complexity. Actual organizational structures are likely to differ in degree from one gang to another. Moreover, the internal structural characteristics often generate the development of different types of groups.

In general, the characteristics of gangs are identified by process, looking at how gangs arise, develop, and interact within their environment. Thrasher (1927) perceived gangs developmentally. In his view, "if conditions are favorable to its continued existence, the gang tends to undergo a sort of natural evolution from a diffuse and loosely organized group into the solidified unit which represents the matured gang...which may take one of several forms. It sometimes becomes a specialized delinquent type such as a criminal gang..." (p. 58). Recent empirical research supports this view of the dynamic processes of the gang. From the Scavenger-type in Detroit gangs of Taylor (1990), to the Puerto Rican "Diamonds" gang described by Padilla (1992), to the majority of Milwaukee gangs studied by Hagedorn (1988), to the Mexican gangs in East Los Angeles described by Moore (1991), all evolved from either dancing or corner groups consisting of teenage friends gathered on corners on their blocks or hanging out together.

As gangs develop more structure to their organization, their function focuses on criminal economic opportunity. Padilla (1992) describes how the "Diamonds" in Chicago organized and became a business enterprise. The gang originally formed as a musical group. Then an incident where one member was killed by an opposing gang led to re-organizing the gang into a violent criminal youth gang. Later it took on a businesslike character. A description by Taylor (1990), who studied black gangs in Detroit, further supports the developmental stage of the gang. According to him, the Scavenger gang enters the stage of the Territorial gang, which then becomes serious about organizing for a specific purpose in its territorial boundaries. When the territorial gang has strong leaders and organizes its structure based on illegal money-making ventures, it stages itself for transformation into an organized/corporate gang. Both Padilla's Hispanic and Taylor's black gangs were linked with adult criminal organizations, when they completed their organizational structure into business enterprises. Researchers, however, like Hagedorn (1998) and Vigil (1988) claim that when gangs are more concerned with fighting and violence, strongly imbedded gang patterns require group effort and support. Klein and Maxson (2001) confirm the view of Hagedorn and Vigil in their report on structure of gangs and types of gang crimes. Klein (1995) also maintained that most American youth gangs are loosely organized and are not involved in the drug business as a whole, although he admitted the existence of drug gangs and individual involvement in the drug business among street gang members.

A quite different pattern of the emergence and development of the Asian gang in Asian ethnic communities has been found. Many Chinese gangs in New York City are emerged with and/or closely associated with adult groups (Chin, 1990, 1996). Although delinquency itself does not necessarily lead to gang membership, Chin (1996) contends that the transformation from delinquent to Chinese gang member is propelled by association with adult crime groups and the internalization of norms and values of the triad subculture. He also theorizes on the social process of gang formation in New York City's Chinatown. The emergence of a new, powerful adult organization is seen as a distinctive factor in the formation of Chinese youth gangs. Social tensions would be produced by the new adult organizations if they challenged both the existing legitimate and illegitimate orders in the community. As a result, conflict between new and existing groups leads to the formation and development of Chinese youth gangs. Based on law enforcement sources, Grennan, Britz, Rush, and Barker (2000) describe a similar pattern of association between the Korean gangs and adult groups in New York City. The Korean Power gang, for example, in Manhattan is affiliated with the Korean Merchant Association, which in fact controls the activities of the Korean Power gang. Another gang, the Korean Flying Dragons, is affiliated with the Chinatown Hip Sing Tong and their associates, the Chinese Flying Dragons.

A recent book by Leet, Rush and Smith (2000) describes the adult group as a part of a Korean gang organization, instead of a network between youth gangs and adult groups. According to this book, Korean crime groups are categorized into three tiers, distinguished by age group. There is an adult division where the age of members runs from 25 to 60. They control the organization and many of them are ex-Korean Intelligence Agency members. A young adult group exists with ages ranging from 18 to 24. This group is extremely ruthless and aggressive; its primary criminal activity is extortion of Korean business. Finally, there is a juvenile group, with ages ranging from 13 to 17 years. They engage in petty thefts and robbery. Although this structural analysis follows the traditional vertical structure of the gang, it differs in its leadership, age range, and size compared to those of other ethnic gangs.

Unlike Leet et al's Korean gang description, which looks like a pyramid of military structure, traditional vertical gangs tend to have their own leadership at each age level, although it varies widely across ethnicity and community, between gangs and over time within each group (Klein, 1995; Thrasher, 1927). Hagedorn (1998), for example, finds that Milwaukee gangs are all age-graded and that each age group has its own "main group," its leaders, and its "wannabes." Moore (1991) observes changes in the age-graded structure of two barrio gangs in East Los Angeles. Suttles (1968) analyzes gangs in Adams area of Chicago in terms of different age groups. The Chinese gangs studied by Chin (1990, 1996) have their own leaders, who maintain direct contact with certain tong elders. Thus, the Chinese gangs do have a sort of affiliation with the adult groups, but the adult groups are not actually considered part of the gangs.

Depending on whether or not adult groups are part of Korean gangs, the size of the gang and the average age of the gang members vary greatly. Moreover, the size and age estimates are heavily dependent on what types of gang members are counted as hard-core members, fringe members, or wannabes (Klein, 1995; Spergel, 1995).

With variation in mind, Thrasher (1927) reports that the size of the gang ordinarily ranges from 20 up to 100, while some have up to 2,000 members. Thrasher's findings are consistent with many studies showing gang membership ranging from 25 to 200 (New York City Youth Board, 1957; Vigil, 1988) to thousands (Miller, 1982; Short, 1976). Chinese gangs range between the ages of 13 and 37 with an estimated membership of 20 to 50 hard-core members (Chin, 1990). Grennan et al (2000) reports junior groups under the control of the Korean Power gang in New York City (excluding adult groups) consisted of youth between the ages of 14 and 30, with an estimated membership of 75 to100. In terms of age range, researchers generally agree that the upper age range of gang members has expanded dramatically (Hagedorn, 1998; Klein, 1995; Moore, 1991; Spergel, 1995). However, depending on adult groups, the age range of Korean gang members can be either broad or narrow, and the average age may be lower or higher.

While some Chinese and Korean gangs have been found to associate with adult groups, many other Asian gangs do not have any connection at all with adult groups. These non-adult affiliated Asian youth gangs include such groups as the Vietnamese, Taiwanese, and Korean immigrant youth gangs which emerged in Asian communities of Queens and Brooklyn (Chin, 1990, 1996). Their primary criminal activities are concentrated in moneymaking operations such as extortion, robbery, and burglary (Chin 1990, 1996; Jackson & McBride, 2000; Vigil & Yun, 1990). Compared to Tong affiliated gangs, these gangs seem to be less organized, smaller in size, younger in age, less cohesive and with fewer ties to neighborhood traditions. Chin (1990) argues that these gangs resemble Cloward and Ohlin's conflict gangs, because they failed to integrate or have not yet integrated themselves with illegitimate opportunity structure and adult criminal elements.

With such a diverse nature of gangs, Yablonsky (1962) suggests a concept of gang as being a "near group." On a continuum of the degree of social organization, he situates the gang midway between the mob at one end and the social group at the other. Generally, youth gangs are seen as loosely organized groups generated in socially disorganized areas where the ethnic concentration effect (Wilson, 1987) is visible. In essence, some youth groups can develop into more organized groups in poverty milieus, illegal opportunity and ethnic cultural setting, while many youth groups maintain their delinquent peer group characteristics only for a certain time period and then dissolve.

Behavioral Characteristics: Gang Proliferation, Drugs, and Violence

A dramatic increase in gang problems has taken place over the last two decades in the United States. Research strongly suggests that the number of gangs and gang members has increased in cities across the country (Egley, 2005; Klein, 1995; Maxson, 1998; Miller, 2001; National Youth Gang Center, 1997, 1998, 1999, 2000). The proliferation of gangs also indicates that the gang problem has expanded to small and medium-sized cities as well (Howell & Egley, 2005). The impact of gang proliferation is critical since gang membership intensifies delinquent behavior (Battin-Pearson et al, 1998; Huizinga, 1996; Thornberry, 1998; Thornberry et al, 2003). When compared with youths who do not belong to gangs, gang members are far more involved in delinquency, particularly violent and serious delinquency (Esbensen & Huizinga, 1993; Fagan, 1996; Huff, 1998; Klein, 1995; Moore, 1991; Sanders, 1994; Short, 1996, 1997). Thus, it is expected that rapid gang proliferation will cause more serious crime problems on the national level. The recent increase in concern about Korean American youth gangs in the Korean communities suggests that they have not been exempt from gang proliferation in the United States.

There are three distinct, but sometimes overlapping, explanations of today's gang phenomenon. The first is the process described as "gang migration." According to the study by the National Youth Gang Center (1997), almost 90% of respondents reported that gang members from other cities had migrated to their cities. Another gang migration study (Maxson, 1998) showed a similar result, finding that 72% of law enforcement agents acknowledged that their jurisdiction had experienced gang migration. Consider next the self-emergence of gangs caused by burgeoning social problems. Gangs naturally arise in cities throughout the U.S. that are characterized as socially disorganized areas due to deindustrialization, rapid social and economic change, and/or the ethnic concentration effect (Anderson, 1999; Fagan, 1996; Wilson, 1987). Finally, the spread of gang culture and public moral panic is engendered by the mass media. Sullivan (2000) links the concept of public moral panic to the gang proliferation phenomenon. His logic begins with the general decline in crime, particularly serious crime, over the last few years. After a comparative analysis of official arrest data in three different neighborhoods in New York, he confirmed the general decline in violent crime after it peaked in 1991. If gangs are spreading widely and have migrated into New York City, bringing with them their involvement in illegal activities, then violent crime should have also increased. Sullivan suggests that the decline is a result of the spread of gang culture and public moral panic interacting with the mass media, rather than an actual gang migration phenomenon. The "cafeteria-style" delinquency among many gangs (Esbensen & Huizinga, 1993; Fagan, 1989; Klein, 1995; Klein and Maxson, 2001) may disguise the actual increase of official violent crime data, thus projecting misdemeanor data. This research confirms it is very unlikely that the recent increase of Korean group delinquency is part of the gang migration effects. Rather, it should be understood in its local context, which will be dealt with in detail later.

As noted, the seriousness of the problem lies not only in the extent of the rapid increase in membership, but also in the gangs' violent character and drug related problems. Historical analysis shows violent crime among gangs and gang members was less common in earlier periods than it is now (Klein, 1995; Moore, 1991; Short, 1996, 1997). There is a problem of measurement, because no comparable data across time and place exists, definitions are inconsistent, and the data demonstrates short-term fluctuations (Fagan, 1996; Spergel, 1995). The cycles of gang homicide now seem to end at a higher degree of seriousness, climbing to higher plateaus before surging forward again. If homicide is an indicator, gang violence has become a far more serious problem during the past decade (Maxson & Klein, 1996; see Pizarro and McGloin, 2006). According to Sanders (1994), the presence and availability of weapons and the use of vehicles in drive-by shootings has contributed to an increase in gang violence. These violent incidents are sometimes planned, but spur of the moment decisions are common (Hughes and Short, 2005). The older age of male gang members has also contributed to gang violence, although the rise in overall juvenile and female violence in recent years has also had an effect (Spergel, 1995). Fagan (1996), Hagedorn (1998), Moore (1991) and Short (1996) also argued that various factors - the spread of gang culture, the masculinity concept, social and economic dislocation, and the perception of desire to outdo their predecessors– are all responsible for the increase in gang violence. According to Chin (1996), gang violence among Chinese gang members- robbery, shooting, and fighting- are due to provocative attitudes, turf warfare, revenge, and money. Grennan, Britz, Rush, & Barker (2000) report that most Korean gangs are heavily armed and engage in extortion, home invasion robbery, protection of prostitution houses, and kidnapping. As we will see, some of the gang activities in Korean communities have changed.

Gang members may progress from gang violence to drug use to drug trafficking, which then becomes a basis for a sophisticated criminal organization (Padilla, 1992; Taylor, 1990). There are, however, significant exceptions to this sequence. Although the prevalence of self-reported delinquency and substance use was far greater for gang youths compared to non-gang youths (Fagan, 1990), there was no connection between violence and drug selling among Chicano, Chinese, and African American gangs (Chin, 1996; Hagedorn, 1998; Moore, 1991). According to Hagedorn (1998), the youth gang's fluid, unstable, emotionally charged character is not suited to a rational drug organization. Howell and Decker (1999) also conclude that although gang members are more active in drug use and sales compared to nongang members, their drug business is somewhat limited in terms of its scale and geography. Thus, it is assumed that drug involvement is usually done individually and sporadically. In spite of this, it is hard to deny the emergence of new youth drug gangs may be due to the availability of drug markets, social and economic change. Based on law enforcement resources, Grennan et al (2000) report that Korean gangs are involved in street sales of various illegal narcotics such as rock cocaine, marijuana and heroin, although they concentrate predominantly on the sale of methamphetamine. Sources from social work agencies and law enforcement (personal interviews, 1998) indicate that Korean American youths are engaged in various illegal activities including selling and using MDMA (club drugs). This research found both delinquent groups and gangs abused various illegal drugs. Selling drugs is popular among individual gang members in Korean gangs rather than an activity participated in by the whole gang. The study found no relationship between drugs and violence among Korean gang members.

IMMIGRATION AND THEORIES OF THE GANG

An early attempt at an explanation of the relationship between immigration and youth gangs is found in the Social Disorganization Theory. This explanation focused on the development of high crime areas in which there is a disintegration of conventional values caused by numerous large immigrant groups who found themselves in extreme poverty, transient residence, and poor housing, factors which resulted in a general lack of stable community institutions. On the assumption that such factors contribute to instability in the immigrant community, an absence of close interpersonal relationships among different immigrant group members, and a breakdown in the effective social control of the behavior of the children of immigrants, social disorganization theorists concluded that high crime "zones" would be disproportionately characterized by social disorganization. From their viewpoint, immigrants who lived in such situations were not necessarily deficient socially; rather they responded to disorganized environmental conditions. This angle of vision links to a key concept, the cultural transmission process through which criminal values and traditions in socially disorganized areas are handed down from one generation to the next among different immigrant groups.

Two Chicago sociologists, Shaw and McKay (1942), studied the concept of social disorganization and delinquency occurring during the early decades of the twentieth century. With long-term observations of changing immigrant ethnic groups in the same high crime areas, they contended that delinquency rates corresponded to neighborhood structure and that crime was the product of local economic conditions, tradition, and values. Ironically, they acknowledged the importance of ethnic differences in crime rates by noting the unusually low rates of delinquency among "Oriental" juveniles. This observation was not developed in their explanation of delinquency and was later contradicted by a large increase in the number of Asian gang members during 1970s after the passage of the 1965 Immigration Law (Miller, 1975). Moreover, various studies identified apparent differences in the types of delinquency due to the distinctive experiences and value systems of particular racial and ethnic groups (Curry & Spergel, 1988; Ianni, 1974; Sellin, 1938; Vigil & Yun, 1990). Social disorganization characteristics often interact with the ethnic cultural traditions which immigrant groups bring to the new land, and then create the basis for certain patterns of gang crime behavior among the children of immigrants. Although social disorganization theory does not specify the distribution of types of gang problems and immigration, it supports the relationship between immigration and youth gangs through which a cultural tradition of delinquency transmitted, developed and continued.

Many children of immigrants in disorganized inner cities area feel isolated, frustrated, hopeless, and often become angry while they go through the acculturation process. Strain theorists attempt to explain juvenile delinquency and gangs as being a direct result of lower-class frustration and anger when confronted with a lack of access to the opportunity and rules of the dominant middle-class culture. As a result, a unique form of group emerges with alternative life-styles and values. This subculture has developed and maintains independent values and beliefs that conflict with conventional social norms. The Strain theories themselves do not directly explain conflict caused by the immigration process. Instead, they try to find the root cause of criminality in the clash of values between differently socialized groups over what is acceptable or proper behavior. Nevertheless, the study of this tradition concentrates on lower-class ethnic groups who are immigrants (Chin, 1990; Jankowski, 1991; Moore, 1991; Padilla, 1992; Vigil, 1990).

This line of study, which establishes the relationship between crime and immigration, can be traced to Thorsten Sellin's classic 1938 work, *Culture Conflict and Crime.* According to him, a criminal event is nothing more than a disagreement over what should be acceptable behavior, and conflicts between the norms of divergent cultural codes "are inevitable when norms of one cultural or subcultural area migrate to or come in contact with those of others" (p. 63). In his work with juveniles, Cohen (1955) reformulates Merton's theory to explain urban lower-class, male gang delinquency. His main thesis is about delinquent subcultures, which arise from the culturally heterogeneous American class system. The gist of Cohen's theory is that not all working - or lower-class boys associate with delinquent peers. Introducing Whyte's observation between corner boys and college boys in an Italian immigrant slum (1937), he explains how lower-class boys join one of three existing subcultures: college boy, corner boy, or delinquency boy. Although his argument that class conflict leads to "formation of reaction" may be accurate, the American class system was never free from the effects of the immigration process itself, because immigrants and their children occupied most lower-class neighborhoods. Cloward and Ohlin (1960) proposed, as did Cohen, that there are three subcultural forms of gangs based on the opportunity structure within a given community: criminal, conflict, and retreat. The form of gang subculture depends on the type of opportunities available in the community and the degree to which the two opportunity structures, the legitimate and illegitimate ones, are integrated. Also, they clearly specify persistence and changes in subcultural forms of gangs with immigration process in the following statement:

Changes in delinquent adaptations also seem to be associated with stages of assimilation of immigrant groups. In the first stage, conflict adaptations abound; in later stages, criminal adaptations appear to be more prominent; finally, as assimilation is completed, violence again tends to break out among those residual adolescent males whose families have failed to rise from the old immigrant slum community. (pp. 45-46)

Researchers also argue that the causal connection between social class and criminal behavior in the strain theory is highly complex since various factors such as race, seriousness of offense, education and inequality of income are involved (Thornberry & Farnworth, 1983; Tittle, Villemez, & Smith, 1978). Moreover, another problem exists that weakens the explanatory power of the strain theory: it does not clearly establish the relationship between social class and the newly developing Asian gangs. Many Asian gang members come from two working parent families, where there is inadequate supervision of the children, rather than insufficient access to income (Chin, 1990; Sung, 1977; Toy, 1992). This factor challenges the assumption of strain theory. In other words, it could plainly be argued that group delinquency among Asian youth peaks during late adolescence, because this is a period of social stress caused by weakening parental supervision and the development of relationships with a diverse peer group, which is intensified in part by the immigration process.

BRIEF HISTORICAL BACKGROUND OF KOREAN IMMIGRATION

The number of immigrants to the United States from Korea has not reached the levels of those from China or the Philippines; but in proportion to the population of their native land, the numbers are truly remarkable. The Korean population in the United States was reported at more than one million in the 2000 Federal Census, making Koreans one of the largest immigrant groups in the United States. Because of the Hart-Cellar Act of 1965, which eliminated national origin as a criterion for immigration in the United States—especially from East and Southeast Asian countries—it has become customary to distinguish between the old immigration and the new.   Bearing in mind the limitations of this classification, we may use it as a basis for discussion.

Scholars unanimously agree that the first group of Korean immigrants to American territory began when 101 Korean laborers arrived in Honolulu, Hawaii, in January 1903.   There was at that time a need for cheap labor on the booming sugar plantations, although a small number of diplomats and students had preceded them (Min, 1995).   According to Jung-Ha Kim (1997), Christian missionaries from the United States played an important part in promoting Korean immigration; the United States Labor Department paid missionaries to give "pulpit service," preaching of the United States as "the land flowing with milk and honey."   In addition to the impact of Christian missionaries, several famines had impoverished Korea, while massive protests by Japanese workers for better labor conditions in Hawaii resulted in their being replaced by Korean laborers.   More than 7,000 Koreans had arrived in Hawaii by November 1905, until the Korean government halted this migration flow because of complaints concerning the treatment of its nationals by the United States (Yun, 1977).

Additionally, the first wave of immigration from Korea was hindered by two historical events: the annexation of Korea by Japan in 1910 and the U.S. Immigration Act of 1924 that eliminated Far East immigration (Kim, 1997).   Within that span of time, 541 Koreans claiming to be political refugees entered the United States, in addition to 1,067 Korean picture brides[2] in accordance with/as established by the gentleman's agreement with Japan.   Practically no Korean immigrants were admitted to America from 1924 until the end of World War II, when Korea declared its independence from Japan.   Other distinctive groups of Korean immigrants include 6,423 wives of United States servicemen and 5,348 "war orphans" who entered between 1951 and 1964, the period of post-Korean War immigration. They are often called an "invisible group," because they are the least studied group of Koreans in the United States (Hurh & Kim, 1984, p. 49).

As was the case with other Asian immigrant groups, the large-scale movement of new Korean immigrants began with the 1965

---

[2] In order to balance the sex ratio among the first Korean immigrants— about ten males to one female— picture brides came to United States between 1910 and 1925.

Immigration Act. According to the 2001 Statistical Yearbook of the Immigration and Naturalization Service from 1950 to 2000, the total number of Korean immigrants who came during the 1950s was 6,231. That number increased fivefold to 34,526 in the 1960s. In the following decade, 267,638 Koreans entered—about an 800% increase. In the 1980s, the number increased again to peak at 333,746, falling to 164,166 in the 1990s. Consequently, it is clear that the majority of Korean immigration occurred during the last 30 years.

Along with changes in U.S. immigration legislation, several conditions in Korea have also influenced the recent phenomenon of immigration to the United States. First, South Korea has experienced tremendous population growth accompanied by industrialization and rapid urbanization since the end of the Korean War in 1953. In an effort to control population growth, the Korean government established an emigration office within the Ministry of Health and actively promoted emigration policies while also focusing on family planning. Second, Koreans were exposed to America through the mass media and the kinship network, preaching the gospel of America as the symbol of a land of opportunity, prosperity, and freedom. Finally, political instability and military tension with North Korea also played a role in the new wave of Korean immigration to the United States; this continues to today.

Contemporary Korean immigrants differ in several significant ways from the first wave during the early 20th century, many of whom came without their families. For the most part, Koreans now come as intact families with the intention of settling permanently and acquiring U.S. citizenship. Nonetheless, many Korean immigrants still have to cope with the separation from their family members for anywhere from a few months to a few years. It is not unusual to see family members stay behind until other member(s) get settled. For example, a husband often comes first, to find a place to live and secure employment. The wife and children reunite with him later.

A large number of immigrants are from the urban middle class of Korean society and are educated professionals (Min, 1995; 2006). The skills and degrees, however, do not easily translate into good jobs in the United States. They frequently find employment in positions far below their training and qualifications because of language difficulties and lack of connections. Such sharply limited opportunities often drive them to seek alternative methods of upward mobility through kinship and other ethnic networks, which has resulted in the current growth of small businesses among many Korean immigrants.

A total Korean population of 1,076,872 was reported in the 2000 U.S. Census. The actual numbers may be greater than the figures indicate because of undocumented and hard-to-document urban populations (Doyle & Khandelwal, 1997). Most Koreans have shown a preference for settling in one of two metropolitan areas: New York and Los Angeles. Koreans in Los Angeles settled west of downtown. In New York City, more than three-fourths of Koreans reside in Flushing, Queens. These areas have experienced urban decline and decay like other major metropolitan areas of the United States. The Koreans have revitalized neighborhoods that were turning into slums only a few years before (Mangiafico, 1988). In spite of their hard work and revitalization of deteriorating urban slum areas, Korean immigrants and their children have to pay a high price for settling in residentially and racially segregated neighborhoods where several contemporary factors, due largely to deindustrialization, already operate directly against inner-city African Americans (Wilson, 1987). Operating a small business and settling in urban centers causes Korean immigrants to experience disconcertingly high levels of violence, which soon become the ordinary routine of lower-class daily life (Anderson, 1999; Fagan, 1998; Miller, 1958; Wolfgang & Ferracuti, 1967). As a result, they often have to bear the burden of victimization and ethnic conflict, particularly with African American residents in their new neighborhoods. The Los Angeles Riot in 1992 is a sad example of the violent frustration at the heart of urban America, which Korean immigrants had to suffer.

EXPERIENCE OF KOREAN AMERICAN YOUTH AND MODES OF ADAPTATION

When young Korean immigrants go through the process of adolescence and immigration, they are more likely to experience adjustment problems than non-immigrant youth. Like all American youth, a Korean adolescent shares the same general difficulties and issues, underlying sociological and biological processes such as physical maturation, cognitive development, moral development, earned and ascribed social status. At the same time, being an immigrant requires living in the cultural margins where old and new come together and they are also faced with crafting an identity that will enable them to thrive in profoundly different settings, such as school and the world of their peers (Lee, 1988; Oh, 1998; Park-Adams, 1997). Based on social context, they develop their identities and styles of adaptation into the new world. Some embrace total assimilation to mainstream American culture. Others incorporate selected aspects of both the culture of origin and mainstream America. Still others reject the institutions of the dominant culture. A recent study on mode of adaptation and delinquency among Korean American youth shows that assimilated youths are more likely to be delinquent than those who are separated or were marginalized (Lee, 1998).

For example, children of Korean immigrants typically come into contact with American culture sooner and more intensely at school, at play, on the streets and through mass media. In fact, they desperately want to be accepted and what is new for them is often what is most desirable. However, their parents are less likely to be exposed to mainstream American culture due to their high level of ethnicity, small business practices that require only a minimum level of English fluency, and also their employment with members of the same ethnic background and/or other immigrants. A survey participated in by Korean American students (n=207) shows 78% are concerned about their parents' limited English proficiency (Park, 1995). As time goes by, the cultural gap between parents and their children creates particular conflicts and tension over two ways of life, the one American and the other Korean, and by the incompatibility of parents and children. The conflict is intensified when children express their acquired American expectations and attempt to transmit them into the family situation. Their parents in turn attempt to reinforce the pattern of the Korean traditional family. Chae (1990) finds that acculturation differences between parents and Korean American delinquent children are larger than those of parents and normal Korean American children. Also, The Korean Family Service Center in New York City reports the generational conflict that affects about 60% of their total cases has to do with the Korean father's authoritative attitude toward family matters ("Generational," 2003). Children are likely to respond to these conflicts by a rejection of the traditional Korean way and that leads to a decline in contact with family and an emphasis on association with others based on peer-group interests. Thus, as the gap between generations increases, age groups become more alienated toward each other (Young, 1973). This peer group association plays a critical role in Korean youth group delinquency; interacting within the urban settlement among Korean immigrants, they are exposed to violence, prejudice, and the inner city subculture.

Of course, not all children of Korean immigrants respond in this manner. They are likely to experience the psychosocial process of negotiating boundaries through which they accommodate both the "old" and the "new" ways of doing things and in the relationships between the generations, interact with people across the boundaries, and finally feel comfortable being themselves (Kim, 2001). However, Korean immigrant youth in the cultural margins are also forced to choose one over the other in their peer associations. They often find they are neither accepted as Americans, nor are they entirely Asian. At the same time, many of them recognize the considerable discrepancy between the American dream that they are taught and the reality that they experience (Song, Dombrink, & Geis, 1992; Toy, 1992). Consequently, they may be drawn to join native minorities in the inner city, adopting an adversarial stance toward middle-class white society (Portes, 1996). As discussed earlier, combining a lack of parental supervision with the pressure of high academic expectations of success, children of Korean immigrants with this adaptation mode may have problems in school and are more likely to drop out, and consequently face unemployment in the formal economy. For many of these children, gangs may be a natural response to seek out a sense of belonging, solidarity, protection, support, and money much like other marginalized inner city minorities (Chin, 1996; Office of District Attorney, 1992; Spergel, 1995; Vigil & Yun, 1990).

In sum, Korean immigrant youths are at risk. Crafting their identity within peer groups is inevitable regardless of their level of assimilation or marginality. Peer group influence is correspondingly great. It is assumed that marginalized Korean youth may join other ethnic peer groups (Porte, 1996), such as Chinese gang associations, or create their own gang formation similar to the Chinese gangs observed in Queens in New York. In contrast, assimilated Korean youth try to find a refuge from the conflicting demands of their other worlds, and so they may form small groups made up of three or more individuals who possess similar interests. These groups may be a particular type of friendship group, which can be seen in almost all communities, engaging in various legitimate and illegitimate activities. Thrasher (1927) defines this group as a clique that "spontaneous interest group usually of the conflict type.... In a certain sense a well-developed clique is an embryonic gang" (pp. 320-321).

CHAPTER 3
Research Method

A robustly designed research proposal is as important for valid and reliable results as is a review of gang literature for the background study of Korean American gang/group delinquency. Research methods utilized in this study include qualitative techniques such as direct observation and specialized interviewing in field studies. Qualitative field research is considered an effective approach in this type of investigation because there is little empirical research on Korean American gangs or delinquent groups in the natural environment of Korean community. The other reason is a cultural and traditional emphasis on the individual as a member of groups to which he or she must not bring shame (Savada & Shaw, 1990). They are less likely to reveal their problems to outsiders and tend to handle the problems in informal and indirect ways rather than seeking professional help through community organizations or claiming their right through the criminal justice system (Pogrebin & Poole, 1990). Thus, neither survey nor secondary data would be appropriate under the circumstance nor would it be scientifically productive.

The section begins with operational definition on the delinquent group and the gang. Details follow about the search process for gang and delinquent group members and the field relationships with them. A description of the data collection method identifies both its strength and weaknesses, and that is followed by a description of the analytical methods and process. Finally, validity and ethical issues are discussed. Examples of a notification form, observation tool, and interview protocols are attached as appendices.

OPERATIONALIZATION

Two different Korean gang-related groups are operationalized in this study. The term "Korean" is applied to both groups as an indicator of ethnic background. The study includes anyone with Korean ethnicity. However, it excludes, for the sake of simplicity, those with combined ethnicities. For instance, if one of his/her biological parents has another ethnic background, the person is excluded from the sampling. It also excludes those who have resided in the United States for less than 3 months, but includes individuals who have resided here for more than 3 months regardless of immigration status. The term "delinquent group" will be defined as any Korean youths of middle or high school age who drop out of school or run away from home, who have experience with other group delinquency but do not have a designated name for their group or do not claim themselves to be gang members. The group must consist of at least two individuals. Although the study measures individual delinquency among members, it excludes individual delinquency when measuring group delinquency.

The definition used by Decker and Van Winkle (1996) is applied to the term " youth gang". This group will be Korean youths with an age range of 14 to 24 who claim themselves to be gang members or have a designated name for their group and who have been involved in a sufficient number of illegal incidents. The difference between the two groups is that youth gang members must label themselves with a designated name or must be labeled by others. Also, the age range of the youth gang is much wider than that of the delinquent group.

To operationalize the causal factors driving group formation and its dynamics, subjects were asked about schooling, family life, friendship, racism, and routine activities. Behavioral factors/indicators/issues such as violence and drugs were selected to measure the scope of the group criminal activity. Since the youth gang is assumed to engage in much more serious crime than the delinquent group, questions are flexible based upon type of group of the interviewee. More details will be provided in the section describing the interview. Their activity is also measured by participant observation, which will be described later.

SAMPLING DESIGN

The target population for this research study is Korean youths and/or young adults who have resided for more than 3 months in Flushing, New York, and Palisades Park, New Jersey. Because this research involves attempting to locate active Korean gang or delinquent group members, the "snowball" or "chain referral" sampling method is used. Maxfield and Babbie (2001) explain this approach plainly for readers unfamiliar with this method:

> ...snowball sampling means that initial research subjects (or informants) identify other persons who might also become subjects, who in turn suggest more potential subjects, and so on. In such a way, a group of subjects is accumulated through a series of referrals. (p. 288)

As Wright and Bennett (1990) indicate, the most difficult part of the snowball sampling technique is locating an initial contact or two. In order to locate potential subjects, I contacted the "New York Korean Youth Center", an agency that provides counseling services to at-risk Korean youths and gang members. Through the counselor in the center, I was permitted to contact one former gang member and one at-risk youth (a wannabe).

A sample obtained through a criminal justice agency has the potential to be highly unrepresentative of the total population of active offenders (Wright, Decker, Redfern, & Smith, 1992). Similarly, most of the cases involving gangs in the Korean Youth Center involve former gang members or those who have served time in prison. The counselor explained:

> Once they are reached by this agency and follow the program offered by the center, 95% of them can be rehabilitated. The problem is outreach to these people. Parents do not admit the fact that their kid has a gang-related problem. Even if they know of the problem, most family members try to hide their kid's problem. When parents or family members realize the seriousness of problem and contact this center, and ask help, most of kids are already out of control by that time.

It took almost seven months to reach active delinquent group and gang members. Various strategies were used to recruit the target population in the study: referral from former gang members and wannabes, direct contact with youths at research sites known as hangouts, Internet recruitment through an advertisement on the popular Korean American Internet sites such as "Korealink"[3] and "New York Seoul"[4]. The Internet advertisement originally seemed to offer a stronger initial contact than through the agency. Since the Internet is popular among young people and provides anonymity, it was expected that new emerging gangs, gang members, at-risk youth and/or someone who knows these people would respond to the advertisement. However, the Internet advertisement turned out to be unsuccessful, although a couple of emails were received from potential gang or delinquent group members.

CONTACTING SUBJECTS AND FIELD RELATIONSHIP

When I first took an interest in Korean youth gangs, I contacted a local Korean newspaper reporter who had covered a couple of Korean gang stories. The reporter informed me of her sources for her newspaper articles and introduced me to the Korean detective, Shim, and the counselor, Lee. It was from them that I gained information about former gang members, although arranging an initial interview was much harder than I had expected.

Based on the information obtained from interviews with former gang members, I was able to identify certain billiard clubs and Internet cafes as the most popular gang hangouts. By regularly frequenting these sites, I had the opportunity to talk with young customers with knowledge about Korean gangs and delinquent groups. Contact information for at-risk youths who had dropped out of school and/or run away from home was also obtained from Korean Youth Center. Whenever I met these subjects, I asked whether I could talk with them. Initially, many of them showed anxiety and suspicion. After a couple of encounters with these subjects, I was usually able to get them talking.

---

[3] I posted the advertisement at the website: http://www.korealink.com/classifieds/announcements/ads/407.shtml

[4] http://206.245.189.171/cgi-bin/mytown/newyork/list/list.cgi?read=4484

Normally, I offered what Spradley (1979) described as "friendly conversation" before any interview. Once they accepted the interview, a notification letter either in English and Korean was read to these subjects.

Well-known gang researchers suggest that the field researcher should spend long hours in the research setting to develop good informants (Hagedorn, 1990; Taylor, 1985). Building up a rapport by maintaining regular contact with gang members is another important factor for the researcher to convince potential subjects to participate in the study. Through the rapport process, the informants also learn who the researcher really is. Most often, a good rapport encourages them to talk about their world. However, I had difficulty finding a New York research site simply because of the distance and travel time from my home. Another problem was the fact that most of the gang/delinquent group members are night owls who are active throughout the night until morning. To overcome these problems and maximize the sample size, I set up the time frame and traveled to the research site almost every weekend night until I managed to contact a couple of good informants successfully. Later, I spent weekdays there as well during the summer for physical and social observation.

The give and take method also plays a critical role in the field relationship between the researcher and gang members (Decker & Van Winkle, 1996; Wright & Bennett, 1990). Every interviewee that I have contacted was informed of my willingness to help him or her as needed. They were also informed of the confidentiality of the research. This is an important factor in this research because current gang or delinquent group members are the subjects of the study.

Other techniques for forging trust such as the language and customs of gang members can help the researcher in obtaining familiarity and closeness (Decker & Van Winkle, 1996; Wright, Decker, Redfern, & Smith, 1992). Further, these aid in the understanding of the gang subculture. I normally wore casual dress at the research site. I bought a pair of sporty black jeans, which are popular among group members. I tried, when they allowed me, to go to nightclubs with them. Whenever I asked about the dress code on these occasions, my informant said there was no such a thing. But he added immediately, "Black jeans with white shirt is O.K." And I followed his advice.

METHODS OF DATA COLLECTION

Participant Observation

As discussed earlier, this research study was designed to explore not only the causation and formation of Korean-American young gangs/delinquent groups but also their dynamics. Participant observation was used as a data collection method to measure the social activities and physical characteristics of the chosen research sites. The gang and delinquent groups will be described in relation to a particular place, role, and context. As in other studies, they were seen as experiencing change or some other state of being as a consequence of their reactions to a particular setting or living condition.

Social and physical observation can be a practical issue. In order to achieve effective and efficient observation data, hangouts must first be identified in order to select the specific research sites. They also can be divided into public and private places. Billiard clubs, Internet cafés, and karaoke establishments are examples of privately owned businesses. Shopping malls, local parks and street corners are examples of public spaces.

Field notes were used to record observational data. In them I recorded the individuals observed, the particular relationships between individuals, the personalities of the people involved, the sequence of actions, a theme, setting, and point of view. These elements were included to supply information or other specific details where necessary and to omit trivial or irrelevant material.

In addition, my experience on the Jersey City Crime Displacement Project guided me in designing a social and physical observation instrument for public spaces (see Appendix B). As Greiner (1994)'s model suggests, I identified the specific features and conditions that were rated as necessary in the observation sheet. The place and date, number of juveniles identified by gender, the initial arrival and final departure times, weather conditions, any events such as smoking, drinking, vandalism, or violence were observed and rated. The features of the physical environment can contribute to crime and disorder as well as to a fear of crime by facilitating the work of offenders and inhibiting non-offenders (Bureau of Justice Assistance, 1993). Therefore, physical observations such as graffiti, litter, broken glass and dead shrubs were rated at the same time as social observations.

While the observation for the private sites was initially to be conducted in the Rainbow Billiard Club in Flushing, New York, there were obstacles in securing access to this place, which met the criterion of having a concentration of gang members and delinquent group members for the target group. I explained the project and asked to use the billiard club as one of my research sites. But the owner denied[5] that Korean gang members hung out in his billiard club. Having failed to receive his cooperation, I approached another billiard site that met the research criterion. Unfortunately, this site also refused to cooperate.

After much consideration, I decided to change my strategy for securing access to a billiard club. Because of my acquaintance with many Korean Americans in the Korean Catholic Church[6] in New Jersey, I had a chance to meet the manager of a billiard club in New Jersey rather than in New York. The criterion for selection of this site was accessibility and identification of a concentrated target population. After explaining the purpose and the design of the research project, the manager assured me of his full cooperation. According to him, some gang members from New York came to this place because it stays open for 24 hours. With his help, I obtained general information on the busiest time of day, the busiest day of the week, and the average age range of the Korean youth who hung out at this place. Based on this information, I set up the time and day for my observation.

Between 8 P.M. and 11 P.M. on every second and fourth Saturday of the month, I visited this location. I watched TV, watched others play billiards, and chatted with the manager. Sometimes I played billiards with the manager and young customers who might be the potential subjects for my research. I observed this site from December 1998 to July 2001 (except for February and April 2000 for personal reasons), and in this time period I met several high school students. They proudly revealed what they knew about gangs and whom they knew in particular gangs. Three of the subjects that I met also worked for Internet cafés. With their cooperation, I was able to observe young Korean Americans in these sites, as well. I visited these locations almost every first and third Friday and Saturday of the month from September 1999 through July 2001. As can be seen in the table 1, a

---

[5] Denial of this fact means, I believe, he rejects my access to this place.
[6] I was a member of this church and worked as a volunteer youth group teacher.

total of 224 site visits for social and physical observation were made
from December, 1998 to July, 2001. Although I made almost an equal
number of visits to public sites in both New Jersey and New York
research settings, I could not do the same for private sites due to the
denial of access.

Table 1 Number of Site Visits for Physical and Social Observation (from Dec 1998 to July 2001)					
	Research Settings		New Jersey	New York	Total
Observation	Public Places	Shopping Mall	6	6	12
		Streets	37	34	71
		Parking Lot	11	11	22
		Community Meeting	2	4	6
	Private Places	Billiard Club	41	13	54
		Internet Café	22	16	38
		Others	8	13	21
Total			127	96	224

Interviewing

The most enjoyable aspect of the research project was that I made my
discoveries by observing the daily activities of Korean youth, by
listening to what young Koreans said to me, and by respecting and
trying to understand their lives. The other data collection method,
interviewing, was used to hear about their world in their own voices.
The interview involves two distinct but complementary modes: the
informal conversational interview (see Appendix C) and the formal
questionnaire interview (see Appendix D). Both were used
interchangeably depending on interview circumstances and the
interviewee's preference. Interviewees also chose either the English or
the Korean version of the questionnaire depending on their language
preference.

I obtained the questionnaires used in the Chinatown gang research
from Ko-lin Chin (1996). His instrument contains both structured
open-ended and close-ended questions, and the formal questionnaire

interview of this study was derived from it. The questionnaire includes demographic items, self-reported delinquency and drug use/sales measures, and items on respondents' perceptions of whether members of their gang/delinquent group participate in various types of gang activities or group delinquency, and their involvement in school or work and family life. Other items asked about include gang/delinquent group structures and roles, gang activities, group delinquency and organization, other gangs/delinquent groups in the area, and conflicts with other gangs or delinquent groups.

When the interviewee showed discomfort or said "no" to the formal questionnaire interview, the informal conversation interview was used. During the formal questionnaire interview process, I sometimes switched to the informal conversation interview mode when an unforeseeable interruption of the interview process occurred. For example, an interviewee showed cooperation initially but became anxious and uncomfortable during the interview. Questions in the informal conversation interview address the same domains used in the formal questionnaire interview: school, family, peer groups, routine activities, drugs, violence, and other delinquent behaviors. Each question begins with what Spradley (1979) terms as "descriptive questions". For example, "I would like to hear about your daily life, from the time when you get up to when you go to bed, in your own words". Based on the interviewee's description, I ask for more details or move to next descriptive question.

A digital tape recorder was used when the interviewee allowed me to record the interview. The best part of the recorder is the Voice Operating Record function. It does not require the interviewer to press any button for operating. It automatically records when any sound is made. Therefore, both the interviewee and the interviewer can concentrate on the interview.

The friendly conversation was used until the subject no longer felt uncertainty or discomfort about the study. In addition, various places were utilized for interviewing to enhance the free flow of the conversation and comfort. Most of these places were selected if their environment provided ethnic homogeneity and a more relaxed atmosphere for the interview. For example, they included Korean restaurants, the manager's office in the Internet café, the billiard club, and my car. If a subject agreed to participate in the study, I always asked whether they had a preferred place for interview.

In an attempt to let interviewees "speak freely using their own terminology" (Wright & Bennett, 1990), I tried to avoid any interruption until the interviewee had finished their turn to speak. Immediately after their turn, I expressed my interest in and ignorance about what they had said, for the sake of obtaining a more in-depth response.   At the end of the interview process, I asked them to summarize or organize what they had told me in their own words. Many of them who met delinquent group and gang criteria were also asked about the possibility of a second interview.   Both formal and informal interviews took about 2 hours each.

Before interviewing each subject, I explained to them the purpose of the study and their rights once they agreed to participate. Two more telephone contacts were made to solicit participation as well as to clarify any concerns about the study. A first interview for two referrals was scheduled on Thursday, October 22, 1998, at the New York Korean Youth Center in Flushing. However, these two people did not show up.   In rescheduling, I arranged to interview them on Tuesday, December 1, 1998, at Kum Kang San Restaurant in Flushing. The third interview was conducted on Saturday, February 20, 1999, at the same place. The fourth interview was conducted Sunday, March 14, 1999, at Woo Chon Restaurant in Manhattan.   Once the interview was completed, each participant was paid twenty dollars. I also told them if they introduced me to other gang members, I would pay ten dollars per referral.

Nine more youths were recruited from the billiard clubs and Internet café. Due to lack of funding, I told them there would be no payment for the interview itself. However, I maintained my practice of giving ten dollars per referral. Four people introduced me to more than eight subjects. A total of 63 youths were interviewed by the end of August 2001 (see table 2). Initially, 52 met the sample criteria when youth at risk were included in the sample. For data analysis between delinquent groups and gangs, a total of 34 gang and delinquent members are included. Since the study also compares two specific youth groups as a case study, the sample size becomes 18, with twelve members from one delinquent group located in Palisade Park, New Jersey, and six gang members from Mo Ming Pai gang located in Flushing, New York. However, for data analysis such as the role of Korean females and associates with groups, subjects who are not gang or delinquent members are also included.

Table 2 Descriptive Data Sheet of Sample Size					
	New Jersey		New York		Total
Gangs (All Male)			*Do Gae Bi* (Ghost)	3	12
			Green Dragons	1	
			Korean Power	2	
			Mo Ming Pai	6	
Delinquent Groups (All Male)	Delinquent Group I	12	Delinquent Group IV	3	22
	Delinquent Group II	5			
	Delinquent Group III	2			
Youth At Risk	Male	3	Male	5	18
	Female	5	Female	5	

METHOD OF ANALYSIS

Analysis involves dividing something into its components and explaining what they are, under the assumption that it is easier to consider and to understand the subject in smaller segments than as a large, complicated whole. Yet analyzing qualitative data is often a cumbersome and lengthy process, because qualitatively oriented participant observation and related case study strategies rely predominantly on the inductive approach of identifying emerging themes and hypotheses. The analysis of this study focuses on *how* rather than *what*. In order to provide good descriptions of how Korean youths form, join and/or develop into different level of gangs within the Korean community context, I utilized the strategies for qualitative data analysis suggested by Maxwell (1996). They are (1) reading the interview transcripts, observational notes, or documents, (2) writing notes and memos on what you see and developing tentative ideas about categories and relationships during reading, (3) using these memos to categorize and contextualize strategies.

Through these strategies, the study identified the stages by which delinquent groups/gangs are created or formed. For instance, I analyzed two types of groups in two different communities by comparing and contrasting how they come together in the first place. It enabled me to explain how the gang functions or works for individual gang members, as well. The analysis also explained the meanings and implications of the concept of "Korean American group delinquency" as the basis for future gang study that will incorporate the study in question. For clarity, I classified all aspects of the analysis and discussed each one separately. Since the concept "Korean American group delinquency" necessarily involves Korean ethnicity, delinquents and group dynamics, it made sense to consider each by itself. After I had done this, I explained how all of the separate elements of the entity fit together.

As described in an earlier section, data were collected through participant observation and intensive interviews. After data were gathered, they were analyzed before further data collection began. The data were sorted and coded by similar events, activities, patterns and themes that occurred frequently. Through open coding, various forms and patterns of the findings were constantly compared with one another. In addition, the recorded interview data were converted into computer files on my personal computer using the software program "Voice Manager". This program copies recorded sound files to the PC and allowed the researcher to classify, search, and edit the files. I faithfully recorded the process and its outcomes in analytic memos.

The research process was logically connected by way of research questions, data collection, and data analysis. Based on existing theories, the interview data, observation data and memos were created and used to identify patterns, comparisons, trends, and paradoxes. While rereading interviews, I wrote short interview summaries. Further questions and inquires derived from matrices, analytic memos, and a periodic review of all the collected data were studied every three weeks.

VALIDITY ISSUES

1. *Reactivity*: Since potential subjects for participant observation (billiard club, local park and Karaoke) did not know the identity of the researcher, the mere presence of the researcher on the sites did not provoke changes in behavior or attitude of the subjects. Even if I were to identify myself as a researcher in an uncertain situation, it is assumed that the initial effects of this information on subjects would diminish over time (Wright & Bennett, 1990). An interview with a Korean youth can be influenced by the researcher or interviewer. In other words, it is possible that he/she may be affected by my

values, theories, and preconceptions while interviewing. In order to overcome this, I practiced being a good listener and let the subjects speak freely on their own terms.

2. *Selection bias*: Selecting a non-representative study group obviously invalidates any attempt to generalize about larger populations. The Korean gangs or delinquent group members that I studied may be considered representative of the target population, especially currently active gang members or delinquent group youth. Since respondents were selected using several different sampling procedures (agency referral, Internet advertisement, and participant observation), I believe that they represent the maximum variation among Korean gangs and delinquent group members.

3. *Truthfulness*: The subjects of this research project are assumed to be active gang members or delinquent group members. This raises the simple question of how I know the subjects are telling the truth about their illegal and violent activities. All of the subjects interviewed thus far were apprised of, and indicated their voluntary involvement, and understand that this study is confidential. Therefore, they do not have any reason to lie. Moreover, I will assess the veracity of an interviewee's accounts through checking for, and questioning, inconsistent responses (Wright & Bennett, 1990).

ETHICAL ISSUES

Does the research harm any of the participants? Do I endanger myself or study subjects in any way? What if I have to face situations such as degradation, brutality, despair, injustice, and exploitation and can do nothing to change the course of on-going events (Inciardi, 1993)? Does the study protect human rights? Questions like these should be examined at the beginning and during the process. In order to address ethical issues, I first proposed the research project and its protection of human rights to the Institutional Review Board of Rutgers, the State University of New Jersey, before the study began. This approval is required for every researcher at Rutgers who conducts his or her study using human subjects.

The confidentiality of the interviewees in this study was secured by using identification numbers, and there was no identifying information linked to any individual participant. Pseudonyms were used in the text when personal accounts are cited. All files containing personal information were stored in a secure place in the researcher's house. The researcher is the only person who can access the files.

Additionally, I obtained a notification form (see Appendix A) from every individual who met the selection criteria and agreed to participate in the study. The notification form includes information about the purpose and general procedure of the study. It states clearly that participants are always free to make a decision to participate in or withdraw from the study. It also indicates that participants who initially agree to participate can withdraw from the study anytime during the research process without having to justify their choice and without penalty.

To avoid undesirable police intervention, I contacted Korean Detective Shim and other police authorities. I negotiated an agreement with them guaranteeing that they would not interfere in the research, and that I would not be subjected to coercion by the authorities.

In case of a serious future crime such as a drive-by, I in turn agreed to report this to the police anonymously even if this statement does violate the confidentiality of my research. My justification of this violation is that there is nothing more valuable than a human life. I cannot save every Korean gang member whose life is in imminent danger, but I believe saving one life is much more important than continuing this research project and ignoring the crime committed.

CHAPTER 4
The Quality of Korean Community Life

This study explores group structure, process, and activities engaged in by Korean delinquent groups and gangs whose members share a life experience, resulting from a sense of common interest and identity. They are seen as experiencing change as a consequence of reactions to or adventures in a particular setting or condition of life. Gangs and other delinquent groups are often described in relation to a particular place or context. Many empirical researches have shown the significance of surrounding social structure influencing gangs and delinquent groups. For example, Decker and Van Winckle's study, *Life in the Gang* (1997), shows that gangs are affected by environmental characteristics. Sullivan (1989) also describes and compares the ecology and demography of three neighborhoods to see if any group variation exists among them.

This chapter attempts to examine social conditions by which Korean American youth are molded in rather different ways. Since individuals in this study act in certain ways because of their relation to persons and groups in their environment, certain facts about the social characteristics of the communities must be explored in order to understand the similarities and differences between the two Korean youth groups in the study. This chapter employs three data sources, 1990 and 2000 United States Census, 1990 and 2000 Uniform Crime Report, and 2000 *Korea Times Business Directory*, to examine community structure and changes at two research sites: Flushing, Queens, New York; and Palisades Park, in Bergen County, New Jersey.

The two Korean communities have many aspects in common. Flushing is situated less than ten miles east of the Queensboro Bridge in Manhattan, while Palisades Park is five miles west of Manhattan via the George Washington Bridge. Since the 1980s, both neighborhoods have seen an influx of Asian immigrants who have settled in the metropolitan New York City area. Both sites are particularly attractive to Korean immigrants who seek to escape the overcrowding and high rent of Manhattan neighborhoods.

The Korean community in Flushing, Queens, was selected for this study because it is the biggest Korean community in the northeastern United States. Flushing was one of the original four towns of Queens and covered the entire northeastern portion of the county. "Downtown" Flushing, centered around the subway terminal at Main Street and Roosevelt Avenue, is a densely developed commercial and residential area. If one visits downtown Flushing, it may seem like strolling through another country, where residents and merchants banter in foreign tongues and characters of Asian alphabets dominate the storefront signs. Even inside the Starbucks on Main Street, menu offerings like Caramel Macchiato, caffe lattes and crumb cake are listed not only in English, but also in Korean and Chinese. The coffee shop, increasingly a staple on street corners across the country, is next to Ameriasia Bank, Shul's beauty salon (Korean) and Luck Joy Restaurant No.1 (Chinese), and RE/MAX Millennium Realty, all with signs in English, Korean, and Chinese.

The other research site, the town of Palisades Park in Bergen County, New Jersey, was selected because it is the fastest-growing Korean community in the northeastern United States. Unlike Flushing's long history of diversity, Palisades Park was almost entirely white until the 1980s. Korean Americans began pouring into the town during the 1990s. With a rapidly growing population of Korean Americans in the community, Korean merchants started opening up retail shops, focusing on the potential Korean customer base. Along Broad Street are businesses with signs written in both English and Korean. According to the Palisades Park Chamber of Commerce in 1999 there were approximately 250 Korean–owned retail stores that accounted for more than 90 percent of the businesses in the town of Palisades Park. Today, if one visits the town, he or she can see numerous retail store signs advertising restaurants, beauty salons, bookstores, and so forth, owned by and primarily serving Koreans. It is not difficult to see that the language of this community is mainly Korean; one is less likely to see English or any other language such as Chinese.

KOREAN POPULATION GROWTH ANDDEMOGRAPHIC CHARACTERISTICS

Like many different ethnic and racial minority groups who come to the United States and often settle in large cities, the majority of Koreans today reside in large metropolitan areas. Queens County, New York, where the research site Flushing is located, has attracted the second-largest Korean population next to LA County in California, including 63,885 Koreans recorded in the 2000 U.S. Census. Bergen County, New Jersey, where the other research site Palisades Park is situated, also has attracted a large number of Koreans during the past ten years, changing its ranking from the seventh to the fourth largest Korean population of any county, with 58,564 Koreans in 2000. An estimated 30 percent increase of Korean population has been observed in Queens County, with a 130 percent increase in Bergen County between 1990 and 2000.

When the change of Korean population is measured on a smaller scale, the two selected research sites tend to show different patterns. Table 3 provides a general comparison of Flushing and Palisades Park in 1990 and 2000. Flushing grew in population by 12.5 percent from 1990 to 2000. Of the residential population of 80,347 in the year 2000, the major racial group is Asian, comprising more than half the total population, resulting in about a 50 percent increase from 1990. In contrast, White and Black populations dropped sharply during this period, indicating 19.6 percent and 33.4 percent declines respectively. The Hispanic population has actually increased about 2 percent but the change is not significant compared to changes in other ethnic groups.

Table 3 Population change from 1990 to 2000 in two Korean Communities (Flushing, New York, and Palisades Park, New Jersey)						
		1990		2000		1990-2000 Change (%)
	Ethnic Group	Number	Percent %	Number	Percent %	
Flushing, New York	Korean	11,442	15.8	12,111	15.1	5.8
	Chinese	10,628	14.7	20,033	24.9	88.5
	Asian	29,057	40.0	43,386	54.6	49.3
	White	35,492	49.0	28,532	35.5	-19.6
	Black	7,008	9.7	4,668	5.8	-33.4
	Latino*	17,081	23.7	17,393	21.6	1.9
	Total	72,080	100.0	80,347	100.0	12.5
Palisades Park, New Jersey	Korean	1,661	11.4	6,065	35.5	265.1
	Chinese	241	1.6	409	2.4	70.1
	Asian	2,910	20.0	7,016	41.1	141.1
	White	10,911	75.0	8,241	48.3	-25.0
	Black	228	1.6	235	1.4	3.1
	Latino*	1,672	11.5	2,813	16.5	68.2
	Total	14,536	100.0	17,073	100.0	17.5

Source: 1990 U.S. Census and 2000 U.S. Census
*Latino population included showing race and ethnicity changes but they do not reflect the percentages of total population. Because the Census asks people separately about race and Spanish origin, Latinos can identify themselves as being white, black, or other.

One thing noticeable in the population change of Flushing is the dramatic influx of Chinese immigrants, who at 20,333 comprised 25 percent of the total population and became the largest ethnic group in 2000, resulting in about an 89 percent increase. However, the Korean population has been relatively stable, from a total of 11,442 in 1990, to 12,111 Koreans in 2000, showing only a 5.6 percent increase. As a result, Koreans residing in the area, who were the largest ethnic group comprising 16 percent of the total population in the 1990 census of the Flushing, now find themselves the second largest ethnic group after the Chinese immigrants.

In Palisades Park, the total population was 35,461 at the time of the 2000 U.S. Census, showing a 17.5 percent increase from the 1990 Census. The table indicates a similar general pattern of population change, showing a dramatic decline in White population. A total of 10,911 Whites, who comprised about 75 percent of the total population in 1990, sharply dropped in number to 8,241 in 2000, resulting in a 25 percent decline. Unlike Flushing, where the Hispanic-origin population showed a 1.9 percent increase, Palisades Park observed a 68 percent increase, from the number of 1,672 in 1990, to the number of 2,813 in 2000, while the Black population shows only a 3 percent increase at the same time period. Since a large number of Spanish-origin population identify themselves as White and their numbers increased, the actual loss of non-Latino Whites would be more significant. However, the impact of the loss of White population was equalized by the rise in the Asian population, mainly by Koreans.

The Asian population in Palisades Park doubled between the 1990 Census and the 2000 Census. Asians comprise 41.1% of the population, with a total number of 7,016 in 2000. Palisades Park saw Chinese immigration increase 70 percent for 2.4 percent of the total population, with 406 residents as of the year 2000. Noticeable is the 265 percent increase of Korean population in the past ten years, from the number 1,661 in the year 1990 to 6,065 in the year 2000. Koreans residing in this area constitute about 35 percent of the total population, making them the single largest ethnic group.

The dramatic growth in Korean population is directly related to history of Korean immigration. About a half million Koreans (497,912) entered the United States during the last two decades. A very high proportion of Koreans in the research sites are also recent immigrants. The 2000 census, which extracted from the sample population in summary file 4, indicate about 85 percent (4,988 out of a 5,902 sample population) of Koreans in Palisades Park are foreign born. Out of these foreign-born Koreans, 55 percent entered the United States between the years 1990 to 2000 and 34 percent entered between 1980 and 1989. This immigration pattern follows the Koreans in Flushing, too. About 88 percent of these Koreans are foreign-born. Out of them, 52 percent entered between 1990 and 2000, and 37 percent entered between 1980 and 1989.

This recent immigration phenomenon possibly leads Koreans to have high levels of ethnic solidarity. For example, they rely heavily on the Korean language. Table 4 shows almost all Korean households (98 percent) use the Korean language at home in both research sites. In addition, 54 percent of Korean households are linguistically isolated in Palisades Park, while 61 percent of them are in Flushing.

However, this data does not represent an individual language preference. Young Koreans, who were raised in the American education system, prefer to speak English. As Park (1995) observed, in many families most Korean children speak English while parents speak Korean. Using different languages between parents and children causes communication problems, which often result in a more serious generational gap.

Table 4 Language pattern among Korean households in Flushing and Palisades Park				
	Flushing		Palisades Park	
Language	Number	Percent	Number	Percent
Korean	3,453	98.7%	1,855	98%
English	43	1.2%	32	1.7%
Linguistically isolated	2,149	61.4%	1,029	54.4%
Total	3496	100%	1891	100%
Source: 2000 U.S. Census				

Other demographics in the two research sites are similar to each other and to the general American population. The average Korean family size is 3.15 in Flushing and 3.37 in Palisades Park. The overall sex ratio is 89 males per 100 females although the sex ratio is larger in Flushing, with 85 males per 100 females as compared to 95 in Palisades Park. The median age in both sexes is 38.3 in Flushing and 32.8 in Palisades Park.

Since criminologists have long recognized that criminal activity is concentrated among youths and males, this census data has been reorganized by age group and gender. Table 5 indicates the largest age group in both research sites is age 36 to 45, which includes 19 percent of the Koreans in Flushing and 24 percent in Palisades Park. The typical age range for youthful criminals is from 16 to 25, which, in the study samples drawn, comprised about 12 percent in both research sites. As will be seen, the major crimes indexed have dramatically decreased in both neighborhoods. However, the misdemeanor arrest data for age group 16 through 24 in the same period increased more than double in Flushing. Moreover, the ethnographic data collected in this study show that a small but significant number of young Koreans are engaged in various group delinquency and gang activities.

Table 5 Korean Population by Age Group and Sex in Flushing and Palisades Park								
	Flushing				Palisades Park			
Age Group	Male	Female	Total	%	Male	Female	Total	%
Under 16	830	707	1537	15.4	601	561	1162	19.7
16-25	555	646	1201	12.0	385	367	752	12.7
26-35	859	755	1614	16.2	628	446	1074	18.2
36-45	918	971	1889	18.9	637	782	1419	24.0
46-55	635	898	1533	15.4	268	454	722	12.2
56-65	512	824	1336	13.4	227	364	591	10.0
Over 66	274	634	908	9.1	131	413	544	9.2
Total	4583	5396	9979	100	2877	3025	5902	100
Source: 2000 U.S. Census								

SOCIOECONOMIC CHARACTERISTICS

The new immigrants came to America with high degrees of education. As shown in Table 6, the educational attainment of Korean Americans is relatively higher than that of other racial populations. Twenty-seven percent of Koreans aged 25 years and older in Flushing and 40 percent in Palisades Park had completed at least four years of college education. In contrast, 21 percent of Whites in Flushing and 15 percent in Palisades Park were college graduates. This percentage drops to 11 percent and 16 percent respectively in both neighborhoods when looking at the Hispanic/Latino population, while 19 percent of Blacks in Flushing were college educated.

Table 6 At Least 4 Years of College Education Attainment (Age 25 and over)		
Ethnic Groups	Flushing	Palisades Park
Korean	27.3%	40.8%
Chinese	32.3%	-*
White	21.6%	15.3%
Black	19.5%	-*
Hispanic/Latino	11.6%	16%
* The population threshold on Summary File 4 is 100. The data is not available because the population of the selected race or ethnic group is less than the threshold(s).		

Along with a high degree of education, Koreans often say the reasons for immigration are to improve their life conditions and to provide better education for their children. In Korea, when students finish their basic studies, many go on to private schools to prepare for the extremely competitive college entrance examinations. The great pressure to do well on this standardized test and the high cost of private education leads many families to decide to immigrate to America. However, the passion for this education continues among Korean immigrants, and the widespread use of private institutions after school in the U.S. is common among Korean families who wish their children to prepare for admission to prestigious colleges and universities. As seen in table 7, a large number of private institutes are registered in the 2000 *Korea Times Business Directory*. Out of a total of 175 private institutes in Queens, New York, 45 of them operate as educational institutes after school and 31 provide a comprehensive academic education. More than half of them are concentrated in the Flushing area. Although the number of institutes is smaller when compared to Queens, Bergen county in New Jersey has a total 67 Korean- operated private institutes. Except for 7 out of 11 comprehensive academies, they are spread out among many towns and cities in Bergen County.

Table 7 Private Education Institutes				
Types of institutes	Queens	Flushing	Bergen	Palisades Park
After School	45	26	4	2
Math & English	28	17	25	4
Art & Music	71	35	27	5
Comprehensive Academy	31	16	11	7
Total	175	94	67	18
Source: 2000 *Korea Time Business Directory*				

This passion for education and the willingness of parents to sacrifice family resources for their children's success led many Korean American children to excel scholastically. For example, many newspaper articles are often published about students who have a perfect score on SATs, have received U.S. presidential honor awards, or have been awarded some other prestigious scholarships. Also, many private institutes advertise lists of students who have been admitted to universities such as Harvard, MIT, Princeton, Columbia, and Yale.

However, the passion for education sometimes becomes excessive among many parents, and expectations of high academic achievement often become a great pressure on many students. Some subjects in this study mentioned they get burned-out due to the stress from their parents regarding their academic performance. They also mention that it is not uncommon for a handful of students in each class to fall asleep at their desks. Moreover, some went to these institutes in order to avoid any conflict with their parents instead of for the purpose of learning. Because many institutes operate late night, they become a gathering or meeting place for young people.

In spite of high educational attainment and passion for education, Korean Americans' median family income is much lower than the median income for the general population. In 1999, the median income for all New York Koreans was reported as $41,982, compared to $51,691 for all New York state families. Although Korean families in New Jersey earned a higher income than those in New York, they have not yet earned equivalent returns in income ($59,913) compared to the general population's family income in New Jersey ($65,370).

Table 8 shows the difference of family income and poverty level among different racial and ethnic groups in both research sites. Koreans in Flushing have been reported as earning much lower incomes ($28,022) than any other race or ethnic groups. For example, a Korean family in Flushing was making on average about 63 percent of the White, 76 percent of the Hispanic, and 79 percent of the Chinese family income. Again, the Korean family income in Palisades Park ($47,683) trailed White family income ($59,063) by 20 percent, although their income is a little bit higher than the Hispanic population ($46,000).

Table 8 Income and Poverty Status of Selected Ethnic groups				
	Median Family Income ($)		Below Poverty (%)	
Ethnicity	Flushing	Palisades Park	Flushing	Palisades Park
Korean	28,022	47,683	21.2	13.2
Chinese	35,282	-*	24	-*
White	44,490	59,063	15	6.7
Black	43,140	-*	8.1	-*
Hispanic	36,926	46,000	18.3	11.1
*The population threshold in Summary File 4 is 100. The data is not available because the population of the selected race or ethnic group is less than the threshold(s).				

As we saw, about 40 percent of Koreans in Palisades Park had completed at least four years of college compared to about 15 percent of Whites; however, the Korean family income lagged even further behind. It is also shown in the 2000 Census that the proportion of Korean families under the poverty level (21.2 percent) in Flushing is higher than any other ethnic groups except the Chinese (24 percent). The poverty level of Korean families (13.2 percent) in Palisades Park is twice that of White families (6.7 percent). Korean families overall fare badly in income statistics relative to other ethnic groups.

In examining further the sources of family income, I found a striking difference due to the unusually high proportion of self-employed workers among Korean immigrants. According to the 2000 Census, about 20 percent of Koreans are self-employed in the United States. This is almost twice as high as the rates of self-employment in the general U.S. population (11.8 percent). This fact is important in understanding how unsupervised young Koreans get involved in delinquent group and gang activities. As Yu (1987) describes in his study of Korean delinquents,

> Most of these youths (85 percent) had working parents: those with at least one parent at home constituted only 15 percent of the cases. Most fathers were either blue-collar workers or operated their own shops, and the most prevalent occupation for mothers was seamstress work, cleaning or helping with a family business (p. 65).

When both parents were engaged in these family businesses and many of them kept open their shops twenty-four hours a day or until late at night, many Korean youths obviously were left alone without parental supervision. The local data also confirms the high rate of self-employment among Koreans, as Table 9 shows the percentage of self-employment by selected ethnic groups in the two neighborhoods.

Table 9 Self-Employed Status Compared with Other Ethnic Groups			
Ethnic Groups	Total U.S. Population	Flushing	Palisades Park
Korean	20.2%	17.5%	14.9%
Chinese	11.6%	9.2%	-*
White	12.9%	7.6%	9.1%
Black	5.6%	2.1%	-*
Hispanic	9.5%	11.5%	10.1%
* The population threshold on Summary File 4 is 100. The data is not available because the population of the selected race or ethnic group is less than the threshold(s)			

Not only the high rate of self-employment of both parents and long hours of operation are factors, but also many Korean entertainment businesses actively operate and attract young, unsupervised Korean youth (see Table 10). Whether the self-employment rate actually reflects Korean owners or managers of these entertainment businesses, many Koreans participate in such businesses. As described in the methodological section, my social or physical observations were made in and outside of some entertainment places to see interaction among the youths and behavioral patterns. The most popular hangout is the billiard clubs for both delinquent groups in Palisades Park and gang members in Flushing. Since there is no billiard club in Palisades Park, members in delinquent groups have to travel about fifteen minutes by car outside of town to visit one.

Table 10 Korean Entertainment Business				
Types of Business	Queens	Flushing	Bergen	Palisades Park
Billiard Club	10	6	2 +(3)**	0
PC Bang (Room)	12 + (2)*	7	8	3
Nightclub & Room Salon	36	28	11	2
Total	58 + (2)	41	21 +(3)	5
Source: *2000 Korea Times Business Directory* *Two PC Bangs are not listed in the directory, but were personally observed. **Three billiard clubs are not listed in the directory, but were advertised in Korean Newspapers				

In Flushing, there are six billiard clubs where many Chinese and Korean gang members get together on a daily basis. Although some Korean gang members travel to billiard clubs in New Jersey to hang out, they usually stay in local billiard clubs. The other popular hangout place is PC Bang (Personal Computer Room). Almost all members of delinquent groups in New Jersey regularly spend a long time in PC Bang while only some gang members enjoy the Internet games. It often has to do with the age of members. The younger the members are, the more the time spent in PC Bang.

The other entertainment places are nightclubs and Korean bars (room salon). There are a total of thirty-six nightclubs and room salons listed in the 2000 *Korea Times Business Directory* in Queens, New York and most of them (twenty-eight) are concentrated in Flushing. In Bergen County, New Jersey, less than one-third of nightclubs and room salons (eleven) operate their businesses for Korean patrons compared to Queens, New York, and two room salons were opened in Palisades Park. Both delinquents and gang members visit nightclubs. However, no one has said they visit Korean room salons as patrons, due to the extremely expensive cost. Nevertheless, some nightclubs and Korean room salons are related to financial sources for gang members in New York. Although gang members in general admit no extortion is available for targeting these places, they manage these places and share the profits, not only in the form of salaries but also in the form of providing alcohol and employment to their members.

CRIME RATES IN KOREAN COMMUNITIES

Crime rates in general have dramatically decreased during the last decade in the United States. This trend is also found in the two counties and the two research sites under study. A total of 165,179 cases of index crime (except arson) in Queens, New York, and 29,408 in Bergen County, New Jersey, were reported to the Uniform Crime Reporting system in 1990 (see Table 11 and Table 12). These figures declined to 64,662 and 16,615 respectively in 2000. Due to the known validity issues on UCR data, we now look closely at the changes of reported crime on the homicide data, which is believed to be the most valid because the consequences of the crime are so difficult to conceal. Like other index crimes, homicide cases dramatically decreased from 308 in 1990 to 112 in 2000. When this number of crimes are transformed into a crime rate, it appears that 15.8 per 1000,000 persons in 1990 drops to 5.0 in 2000 in Queens County. Bergen County reports 10 homicide cases in 1990 and 3 cases in 2000. Compared to the Queens County's homicide rate, crime rates in Bergen County are about ten times less. The crime rate for this number is 1.2 in 1990 and 0.3 in 2000. The homicide data confirms the general decline of serious crime rates in the last decade. Every index crime category in Flushing has also dropped, from a 30 percent decrease in aggravated assault, to a 70 percent decrease in homicide, in terms of crime rate change when the year 1990 is compared to 2000.

Table 11 Number of Offenses and Crime Rates in Flushing, 1990 and 2000					
Crime Type	1990		2000		% of Change in Rate
	Number	Rate*	Number	Rate*	
Murder	18	24.9	6	7.4	-70.2
Rape	32	44.4	22	27.4	-38.2
Robbery	1045	1449.7	496	617.3	-57.4
Aggravated Assault	406	560.5	301	374.6	-33.1
Burglary	2965	4113.5	1154	1436.2	-65.0
Larceny	1900	2635.9	867	1079.0	-59.0
Auto Theft	4527	6280.5	1645	2047.3	-67.4
Total	11354	15751.9	5264	6551.5	-58.4
Source: UCR and NYPD CompStat *Per 100,000					

However, this dramatic change is not observed in non-serious crimes. In fact, these non-serious crimes increased among young offender groups during the same period. For example, when arrest rates for non-serious crime by age group were examined, there were a total of 169 arrests for misdemeanors between ages sixteen through twenty in 1990. This number increased to 415 in 2000. For the age group between twenty-one and twenty-four, the number of arrests also increased from 158 to 256 for misdemeanors.

Table 12 Number of Offense and Crime Rates in Palisades Park, 1990 and 2000					
Crime Type	1990		2000		% of Change in Rate
	Number	Rate*	Number	Rate*	
Murder	1	6.8	0	0	-100
Rape	0	0	0	0	0
Robbery	5	34.3	6	35.1	2.2
Aggravated Assault	3	20.6	11	64.4	212
Burglary	127	873.6	53	310.4	-64.4
Larceny	163	1121.4	119	697.0	-37.8
Auto Theft	63	433.4	25	146.4	-66.2
Total	362	2490.4	214	1253.4	-49.6
Source: UCR *Per 100,000					

The offense categories that accounted for most juveniles arrested under age eighteen (per 100,000 persons aged ten to seventeen) in Queens County from 1994 to 2000, were robbery, larceny, simple assault, fraud, vandalism, drug abuse violations and disorderly conduct. Out of these offense categories, juveniles were arrested the most for drug abuse violations, which also continue to increase from 2,254 arrests in 1994, to 3,567 in 2000 (data not shown).

In Palisades Park, there was a sharp decrease in property crimes from 1990 when compared to 2000 data. As in Flushing, table 12 shows that burglary and larceny rates decreased more than 60 percent. Auto theft also decreased about 37 percent. However, unlike Flushing where a significant decrease in every index crime has been reported, Palisades Park experienced an increase in violent crimes in index crimes; particularly aggravated assault increased over 200 percent when comparing 1990 to 2000. Since a very small number of incidents of homicide and rape (a total of less than ten reports during the last fifteen years) were reported, the number of robberies and aggravated assaults is projected for fifteen years to see their crime trends in Figure 1. Palisades Park's violent crime appears to have bottomed out in 1987. Then it goes up every year (except from 1990 to 1991, when no change is made) until it reaches its peak in 1995, followed by a decline for the next two years in 1996 and 1997. The total number of violent crime again goes up in the following year, close to its peak. It appears that violent crime reported to police has stabilized, but at its high level in 1999 and 2000. The aggravated assault statistic continuously rises from 1985 to its peak in 1996. For the year 1997, immediately following its peak year, the number of aggravated assaults drops about 33 percent from twelve cases in 1996 to eight. Then, it again increased more gradually for the following three years. The robbery statistic is difficult to interpret due to its fluctuation throughout the fifteen-year frame, but it seems the pattern of robbery increased overall.

Figure 1 Violent Crime Trend in Palisades Park From 1985 to 2000

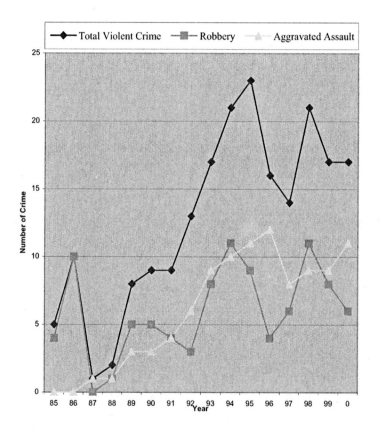

Crime data here is presented to describe the similarities and differences in the two Korean communities in terms of the general pattern of crimes. However, they do not explain group behaviors among Korean youth. There are many variables, such as language, education, and economic activity patterns that are discussed in this chapter, all of which reflect social forces that lead to quality of life within Korean-American communities and their life-style. All these variables are inevitably related to the process of immigration, through which young Koreans adopt different levels of adaptation that create different pools of young people to get together in different community contexts where they develop and join different types of delinquent groups and gangs. Now we shall turn to the immigration process among Korean youth in the following chapter.

CHAPTER 5

Assimilation: Comparison of General Characteristics of Delinquent Groups and Youth Gangs

The life structure of Korean immigrants in communities becomes directed into unique patterns through the immigration process described in the preceding chapter. A large number of Koreans who are foreign-born and recent immigrants tend to maintain a high level of ethnic solidarity although they partially adopt American life-styles. However, the children of Korean immigrants are rapidly assimilating into the American value system. They are socialized under the influence of two different cultures. Their actions and attitudes are molded both by the Korean group and by the American community at large. By the latter, they are pushed into conformity with American culture; the former cooperates to some extent in this process, but also trains them to conform to Korean culture. As a result, they acquire habits and attitudes that conform to two cultures. In some cases, young Koreans must choose only one culture consistently because certain traits are incompatible. In other cases, they can follow two alternative sequences of behavior at different times, although these cannot appear simultaneously. In still other cases, they assimilate the values and norms of the culture of another particular ethnic minority group in the community, for example, the Chinese.

Each assimilation process greatly influences the young Koreans to create their self-identity and sometimes to form themselves into delinquent groups or youth gangs accordingly. In addition, individual experiences within the life of delinquent groups or youth gangs reshape or affect significantly the individual's self-identity. This chapter will examine the general characteristics of delinquent groups and youth gangs based on the different types of assimilation processes among young Koreans.

ACCULTURATION: FOBBIES AND TWINKIES

Young Koreans in general tend to segregate themselves into a form of youth group based on the assimilation process. This phenomenon is also observed in Korean delinquent groups and youth gangs. Here, they are classified into two distinct types: Twinkie and Fobbie. The first is composed of a small number of young Koreans who strongly identify with the dominant mainstream culture. Others recognize them as "Twinkies." The term "Twinkies" often conveys a negative meaning of dual identities, in which they are Koreans but display themselves as American. The majority of members of this type were born in America or migrated with their parents when they were very young. The members of this group try to rid themselves of habits and associations that mark them as Koreans and try to become, as completely as possible, American. However, because the Korean portion cannot be completely erased or forgotten in white, mainstream America as they grow up, members usually get together without their American fellows or associate with other Asian friends. Despite the awareness of their Korean portion, they display rather consistently American values. They communicate with one another in English all the time, although some of them do speak Korean. In fact, none of the Twinkies in this study gave their interviews in Korean when they were asked which language they preferred.

The Twinkies either develop small-size delinquent groups or join Chinese gangs. The Twinkie type of delinquent groups identified in this study usually have groups that are limited to two or three individuals. Since members realize that their skin color cannot disappear in white American society, they report some non-Korean friendships, but draw a distinction between their best friends and their other friends and say that the former have all been Koreans. For example, a member told me: "All my best friends are Koreans. I believe I told you this before; I have a variety of different friends. I have Hispanic, white, and Chinese friends. But, I believe, mostly Koreans now." These groups sometimes engage in violent fighting but usually tend to avoid any violent contact with other groups. Drug abuse was their most common delinquent behavior.

Six Korean-affiliated Chinese gangs were identified by Twinkie participants in this study when they were asked if any gang they knew had Korean members. The gangs they identified are Mo Ming Pai, Green Dragons, Ghost Shadows, Korean Taiwanese Boys, Korean Flying Dragons, and Korean Fuk Ching gang. Sometimes they develop their own Korean factions of Chinese gangs when more Korean members join; their gang names, such as Korean Taiwanese Boys, Korean Flying Dragons and Korean Fuk Ching gang, indicate this. Many Twinkie-type members who joined Chinese gangs had a previous experience with Korean gangs. However, being highly assimilated in American culture prevents them from remaining in the Korean gangs where Korean custom-respect is strongly enforced. In Korea, respect for others according to seniority is a pillar of its Confucian tradition. Seniority is based on age, position in the family, job position, being a teacher, and the list goes on. Confucian tradition demands that the elderly be treated at all times with the utmost respect, whereas "friends" really means those born in the same year who are, therefore, the same age and capable of being equal. As two members illustrate in the following statements when they were asked why they shifted from Korean gangs to Chinese gangs:

> When I hang out with KP (Korean Power gang), I was younger member there. I wasn't familiar with showing respect to Korean elders. I didn't like that. I was brought up American, you know. Like I didn't like giving respect to people I didn't want to give respect to, you know.... It's not fun when you just have to be quiet all the time because you are younger.... I enjoy hanging out with my Chinese friends more than hanging out with Korean people and showing respect to people that I don't wanna show respect, stuff like that. Koreans are more like that and Chinese people more loose. Even though they (Chinese members) are older, you could be more free with them.

> In Korean gang, there is more discipline in various forms. They are strictly enforced and obedience (obeyed). I am "Suhn-Bae" (an elder) and you are "Hoo-Bae" (a younger) which is strictly enforced. If I'm eighteen and you're nineteen,

no matter what kind of action that I provided to the group, I'd be considered as Hoo-Bae, you're Suhn-Bae because of the age difference. In Chinese gangs, ages are not really recognized. Because of this, say that younger group (in Korean gang) recognized all the older members as "Hyung" (another term for an elder) or leaders.

The study successful recruited Korean members from two Chinese gangs: Green Dragons and Mo Ming Pai. Due to only one member of the Green Dragons being available, the Mo Ming Pai gang, from which six members participated in the study, was selected for the in-depth case study. In chapter 7, more details about Mo Ming Pai, a Korean-affiliated Chinese gang, such as process, structure, and activities, will be provided. It is worth noting that no Korean gang members classified as Twinkies in this study ever had membership in Hispanic or Black gangs. Participants also reported none of their Korean friends affiliated with other racial groups except for Chinese gangs.

The second type of Korean youth group develops an adversarial stance toward mainstream culture and tends to identify more with Korean culture, which leads them to affiliate with the Korean instead of the American portion of the community. Most of them consist of young Koreans who immigrated with their parents when they were teenagers. They call themselves "Fobbies," a name that is also recognized by others. The term "Fobbies" originated from "Fresh Off the Boats." For that reason, another term, "FOBs," is also used to describe these groups. Many of them are proud of being "Fobbies" regarding their "Koreanness." But the term also conveys a negative image to outsiders especially Americanized Korean youths like the Twinkies. For example, listening to Korean pop music, or speaking the Korean language to one another in public is considered a "Fobbie" thing to do.

Members of the Fobbie-type groups generally find it difficult to interact with other ethnic friends whose values they do not share; therefore, they usually select friends from the Korean youths whose values are congruent with their own. One member said, "I understand Koreans better than I do other nationalities or races. It's natural. It's very unusual to see a Korean around with Blacks and Whites. I guess they have the same idea 'cause they seem to understand better one another." He also added, "If you get into problems, it's easier to straighten them out with someone of same nationality." When he was asked if he had any problems with other ethnic groups, he continued: "Not really, they don't talk to me and I don't talk to them." In fact, more than half of participants classified as Fobbies were interviewed in Korean, although most of them speak fluent English.

Similar to the Twinkie types of Korean youth groups, Fobbies also form either delinquent groups or gangs. There are two delinquent groups and two Korean gangs identified in this study. One of the delinquent groups, from which all twelve members participated in the study, was selected for the in-depth case study. As described in chapter 6, they participate in various delinquent group activities, but concentrate on fighting and drug abuse. The other delinquent group is similar to the one selected for the in-depth case study in that it, too, identifies with the Korean culture. However, the group differs due to its members' non-immigration status. They consist of members who were sent to America for study abroad when they were teenagers and who are considered as a distinct international Korean student group. These group members usually stay to themselves, or live with their relatives, or otherwise use homestay programs with a host family without their parents, who occasionally visit them from Korea. They also go back to Korea during summer and winter breaks. Some members in the study mentioned they visited Korea five to seven times each year. Many of them come from wealthy families in Korea. For example, some members are simply carrying out rebellious expressions with rigor when they attack international Korean student groups who spend large sums of money and have fancy cars. As a U.S-born youth states:

> In this country, everyone works hard. You get nothing free. But, they're like the king of the world, you know. Never work, but spend money as much as they want. Shithead, retarded kids in Korea. They come here and do nothing but spend what their hard-working parents work for.

The members in this category typically engage in heavy alcohol consumption and fighting and some have serious gambling problems.

There are two Fobbie-type Korean gangs identified in this study. In addition to having a name for the group which is the operational definition in this study between delinquent groups and gangs, the Do Gae Bi gang is involved in more serious criminal activities such as using axes in case of conflicts with other groups, although they resemble other delinquent groups in terms of their structure (loosely

organized) and activities. The other, Korean Power gang, has been
known to Koreans in both research sites and is well organized.
Although a member, thirty-two years old and an alleged leader of one
of three factions separated from the original Korean Power gang,
complained about lack of respect among young members in his faction,
the gang with its membership exclusive to Korean ethnicity is heavily
influenced by Korean culture. As he explains, "When drinking with
Suhn-Bae (old members), we turn our head away to take a drink. If
smoking, we always ask Suhn-Bae to get their permission. You don't
see this respect from young members today. They don't care or listen
to you." However, my social observation confirmed that young
members still follow Korean customs. For example, instead of waving
their hands as a greeting, they bowed their heads when greeting this
older man, and repeated this again when saying "goodbye." The depth
of their bows convinced me that the young people offered their highest
respect to him. The following section of general characteristics of
Korean gangs will describe various Korean Power gang activities and
comes from two in-depth interviews with the faction leader. He asked
me not to interview any of his members, promising that he would talk
with me as much as needed and provide detailed Korean Power
information I requested from him.

So far, I have classified Korean youth groups into Twinkies and
Fobbies to see how they differ based on the assimilation process. It
should be noticed that classification based on the assimilation process
is not always clear-cut. For example, out of a total of twelve members
in a delinquent group, seven exhibit primarily the "Fobbie" reaction,
but also a good deal of the "Twinkie" reaction. In the following pages,
these Korean youth groups will be reanalyzed based on the operational
definition, delinquent groups vs. gangs, and the community context.

DELINQUENT GROUPS IN PALISADES PARK

Members from three delinquent groups participated in the study, while
no gangs were identified in Palisades Park. Generally, the delinquent
groups reveal three interesting sets of characteristics: no self-claim of
being a gang, easy drifting in and out to other delinquent groups, and
no neighborhood exposure to gangs.

No Self-claim of a Gang

None of the members of the three delinquent groups calls themselves a gang. They also insist that no gang label be attached to them. Moreover, in answer to the question, "Are you a gang member?" members who participated here uniformly answered in the negative. In some members' elaborations of this negative response, the general character of the delinquent groups may be seen quite clearly. It is perhaps clearest in the following statement:

> We are not a gang and none of us gangsters. How can we be a gang? I mean for us, we're just friends and brothers who hang around together. It's like I hang out with older brothers for fun and to chill out. That's all.

This denial indicates an attempt to emphasize friendship and kinship characteristics and not to claim anything in a way that might bring aggressive criticism from outsiders. A number of other responses indicate a tendency of downsizing the delinquent characteristic of the group, and a negative view toward gangs. When I used the term "gang" for a delinquent group in Palisades Park, New Jersey, a member revealed his hostility toward me:

> Please give me a break. It's not like the movies, but if you wanna say we are a gang, at least we've got to have a territory, or take control over drugs, colors, stuff like that. Have you seen us do anything like that? I am sorry, but you haven't seen it, have you? Then, prove it, prove it, Mr. Gazebo!

In describing what the gang is, he is adopting the public image of a gang as dramatized through the mass media in terms of what gangs supposedly do. Despite some evidence of group sustenance, membership, and their engagement in various delinquent activities, members of the groups mark off their group from the image of a gang with their own logic.

Drift In and Out

When the fact that members usually display negative attitudes toward one another is considered, it is ironic to observe that members of each delinquent group easily drift in and out to other groups. They emancipate themselves from the group to which they belong and enjoy their ability to move freely. Nonetheless, it should be viewed as all right to maintain "dual status" instead of to completely dissociate oneself from the group. It means that a group member maintains his membership with the group while associating with members of other delinquent groups identified with his assimilation status. Drifting in and out is possible through pre-existing peer networks, which had been established before members joined the group. Usually, a "drift-in" is made when a member is invited to a party or social recreation with other delinquent groups after which the drift-in member can associate with them. In the following statement, one member explains how drift-in can happen.

> It's HoJune's birthday party. He is kind of an old school friend. I met him with a bunch of his friends at Star (billiard club). He said, Do I want to come down to Manhattan tonight? So, I chilled out with them. It was quite good, actually. I took one and half an E [Ecstasy] but, it's more of a... it's the new people...it's more the event that keeps us going, you know. Then, I kind of would hang out with them when Manho (member in his original group) says there is nothing to do.

The statement refers both to the fact that the drift-in with the other group has happened without a conscious decision, and that association with the original group has been maintained but limits itself to contact with a couple of members. By this time, one's interests and the amount of time spent shift dramatically to the other group.

When members were asked the question, "What do you think about hanging out with people other than your group?" the responses varied but the one most frequently given was nonchalance and considering it as a member's own business.

I don't care as long as he doesn't mess up with us. I was very upset when Eugene didn't show up when we were going fishing. I thought he was with other boys but he called me and said, the baby's sick [a three-year-old sister] and he had to go to the hospital with his grandparents (who don't speak English).

Honestly, I've never bothered who they hang out with--Fort Lee, Ridgefield, even Flushing guys, it really doesn't matter to me. There's always something going on with young brothers. I don't want to get into it every single time.

These statements are quite explicit that individual members can associate with any group of their own choice and the association with other groups makes no difference to the group itself. Thus, the dual status is maintained when the member proves a concomitant ability to play a different role in each group, and is treated with indifference by members of both groups.

No Korean Gang Exposure in Palisades Park

Part of the self-description of their delinquent groups carries implications about the level of exposure to Korean gangs in Palisades Park. These implications are contained in their generalized expressions about gangs when they differentiate their groups from the gang instead of comparing their groups with actual neighborhood Korean gangs. It is worthwhile considering separately their acknowledgment of Korean gang existence in Queens, New York, and their contempt for Korean gang affiliation claims from any Korean youth in their neighborhood in New Jersey. Their knowledge about Korean gangs in New York may be seen here in the following conversation with a member who replies that he was interested in joining the Korean gang.

Joong: Well, at one point, they got everyone's attention. KPs (Korean Power gang), Fuk-Ching, White Tigers, and Dragons, you name it. But, KP was the one I wanted to get in. Now, they are kind of died out, but you know, the KP is still live and kicking. Ex-KP members and young KPs, they run a lot of shit like gambling, blackmailing, and chilling out in

Manhattan and Flushing ...and Long Island, too.   Flying
Dragon was popular but I had no interest in'em.

KS: When you say blackmailing, what do you mean?

Joong: I mean like they go to stores, and ask money for
running business in their territory.

KS: Some of the gang names you mentioned are Chinese
gangs, aren't they?

Joong: Yep, but you know what, a lot of Korean kids join
Chinese gangs because they are more established.

Although some members had a detailed knowledge of Korean
gangs in New York, their denial to a question about the existence of
Korean gangs in New Jersey was uniform in almost every case. As
revealed in the following statements,

> You see, KP members came over here for whatever reasons; it
> is like we go to nightclubs in Manhattan. They come down
> here, too. We go to Flushing to see girls, or for no reason. It's
> same thing with them.   They come over here to see their
> friends, or to have a fun. But you know they do not belong
> here. It is Manhattan or Flushing stuff. Definitely not here.

> The thing about KP here is that you got to take a look at the
> 7th grade or 8th grade young funky honky copycats...there are
> like a couple of hundred kids with the same haircut, the same
> baggy jeans, and they all wear a white T shirt. It is like they
> are everywhere. They're just like acting gang stupidity to
> each other but nothing much has changed...after all, a copycat
> is a copycat. All I see is show-offs, not a real gang.

KOREAN GANGS IN FLUSHING

Members from four different gangs participated, while three members
from one delinquent group were interviewed in Flushing.   Given the
fact that the principal data was collected from the five groups, the
general characteristics of youth gangs in Flushing begin with the
coexistence of delinquent groups and gangs in the community. Thus, I

will discuss organized Korean gangs, the influence of the Chinese gang subculture, and the fact of no public gang identity with names.

Coexistence of Delinquent Groups and Gangs

When characteristics of the groups in Flushing are looked at, the first thing to be noticed is the coexistence of delinquent groups and gangs. Three participants in the study hung out together and formed a group without a specific name. They are one of the two identified Twinkie-type delinquent groups in the study. Like other delinquent groups in Palisades Park, they do not claim their group as a gang. Overall, the group is less organized and more ephemeral when compared to the four gangs identified in the community. For that reason, the existence of delinquent groups is likely to be passed over and not given due attention in the community. If any, the concern would be that delinquent group members are future potential gang members either by their own choice or because of a gang's recruitment. A parent, who participated in a community meeting, expressed his concern about this issue:

> Like we all did when we were young in Korea, I believe it was usual that young schoolchildren did bad things when they were together. However, I can tell that the gangs we see in our community are different. We used our fists to fight our neighborhood boys, but they use guns to kill one another. We stole fruits in neighbor orchards because we were hungry or for fun, but we never burglarized our neighbors or robbed businessmen. I got a call from the police department one day because my son had been arrested with his friends. Later, my son told me he and his friends had to fight against a group of gang members. I know my kid and his friends are not gang members. Of course, they are not good kids, either. The thing that really bothers me is there is a great possibility for my son to join the gangs because they are all around us on the street, in the school, PC Bang, and everywhere.

Parental concern about the presence of gangs and young Koreans' exposure to gangs in the community is seen here. This statement indicates not only that many Korean parents are aware of gang activities and other gang problems in the community, but also that they try to differentiate delinquent groups from gangs. It further suggests that delinquent boys become gang members if they constantly interact with gang members in the community.

Indeed, three delinquent group members admitted that they knew at least one or two gang members personally and hung out with them sometimes. Despite their casual association with gang members, they denied their gang membership either directly or indirectly. One informant said, "Because of people we were with or places we were at, people think that we are a gang." He went on to speak of his personal feeling about gangs, and of his setting out to manage it for himself by avoiding gang membership.

> When I am with them, I don't think anything about gangs. I also try to guard myself against any situation that might say that I am a gang member. If they ask me to join them, I simply say 'Why do you want to bring it up now? I'll tell you if I want to.'

The fact to be noted here is that the delinquent group member is conscious of his vulnerability to gang membership, and that his words "if I want to" is evidence of his effort to overcome the vulnerability of immediate circumstances. Yet the general desire to become a gang member may be seen in many responses, and the other delinquent group members give extended answers that show clearly their willingness to belong to a gang. One reported,

> I wanted to be with them if there was a fight or a meeting. But often what I heard was after things happened. I asked, 'Why didn't you give me a call?' Then they said, 'Sorry, I forgot.' They never think of me as a part of them that they need me. All I do is hang out with them, just like anyone they see in the pool hall.

Overall, the coexistence of both groups in the community implies a great vulnerability for a delinquent group member to be a gang member. It appears that the resistance to gang membership among delinquent group members is by avoiding any conversation regarding gang membership. In some cases, the willingness for delinquent group members to be a part of the gang is seen, but somehow ignored and forgotten.

Organized Korean Gangs: Korean Power

One of the most frequently asked questions in gang studies is, are gangs organized? If they are, how are they organized? This study measured the level of organization of the Korean Power gang, the best-known and most exclusive gang in the community, through its structure and activities.

The principal data employed here are the intensive interviews with two informants. Tae-Ho currently runs one of three factions of the Korean Power gang, worked for the founder of the gang for a while, influenced street leaders during that time, and had the same degree of respect from street leaders as they had for the founder. Jim is a Korean Power member in another faction.

The structure of the Korean Power gang is similar to tong-affiliated Chinese gangs, due to the gang leaders' association with Korean businesspersons. However, it is unlikely that the Korean Power gang is under the influence of the Korean Merchant Association. According to Tae-Ho, the founder of the Korean Power gang protected a few places of Korean entertainment such as nightclubs or room salons, owned by Korean businesspersons who probably were members of the Korean Merchant Association. The gang leader himself never owned his own business nor had membership in the Korean Merchant Association.

Under the founding leader, the Korean Power gang heavily engaged in extortion and gambling. Tae-Ho recalls that the gang used to regularly extort Korean-owned businesses and collected about $20,000 per month, ranging from $50 to $200 from each Korean retail shop or restaurant per month, on thirty-two streets in Koreatown in Manhattan and Flushing. However, at the time of this research, both informants testified that there is no longer any faction involved in collecting protection money from Korean merchants.. In addition, they are convinced that no Chinese or Korean gangs they know of are extorting money from businesspersons. The extortion practice was discontinued after a heavy police crackdown on Asian gangs in New York City, and an attitude change on the part of Korean shop owners during the mid-1990s. As Tae-Ho says, "With all the crackdown, extortion is practically eliminated. If you do this today, Korean owners pick up the phone and call 911 right away." He also remembered that the gang used to run illegal gambling activities and that the founder sometimes set up a gambling house. Some of the members guarded the house and collected debts from gamblers. However, Tae-Ho claims, the leader did not like any of the members to use or sell drugs.

Today, group activities vary surprisingly, based on the leadership. There are currently three factions of the Korean Power gang. It seems that each faction is now separated from the original Korean Power and runs independently. Tae-Ho's faction does not have any name. Two factions still use the name Korean Power, but one faction is inactive due to the faction leader's arrest and conviction on kidnapping charges. When he was asked about his own activities, Tae-Ho constantly compared himself with the founder:

> It is basically the same what Oyaboong used to do it. I am managing the Korean pub. Oyaboong took care of at least one or two (Korean) nightclubs or room salons. He got commissions from the owner and sometimes supplies liquors to these places, too. But I am employed here. Sun-Hee (business manager) recruits waiters, chef, and other helpers. I hire my young brothers as guards and they get paid.

He also said that managers, as with other Korean entertainment places such as nightclubs, room salons, and pubs, are always females who often preside over the daily operation of business with him and his young members. Since he used the term "Oyaboong," the term used for the leader of Japanese organized crime, when he indicates the founder, and uses "organization" for the KP gang, he was asked whether this had any special meaning. He replied, "Since the Oyaboong engaged in a couple of illegal enterprises and fed his young brothers, I call it an organization."

Although Tae-Ho denied any illegal activities, he provided other types of illegal activities committed by several individual members:

> As far as I know, Khwang-Soo (another faction leader) heavily engages in street drug selling and insurance fraud. He is like Yyang-ah-chi (junk dealer) and street smart. He has never served any prison terms. His brothers (young members) were sent to prison instead of him. That is why Oyaboong did not see Khwang-Soo's boys as a part of the organization.

Jim confirmed Tae-Ho's story. "He (Khwang-Soo) always has a lot of amount of drugs. I don't know where he gets them. A couple of us cut it and sell it on the street." When Jim was asked about the operation of insurance fraud, he continued:

I was involved in it just once. Two cars are used in the scam and it is simple. Once we target a car (for insurance fraud), the leader (Khwang-Soo) and his girlfriend (whose race is white) approach the target driving at a high rate of speed. Usually, the target accelerates to keep distance. At that point, we (the other car) cut in front of the target and slam the brakes. The target runs into the back of the car and all of us in the car claim to be injured. The leader's car stops also. Soon the police arrive and begin to question everyone involved. All of us claim that the target was speeding and recklessly drive into the rear of our car. The leader's girlfriend also tells the police that she stopped because she was a witness to this reckless event.

Tae-Ho mentioned the operation of massage parlors, but he denied the group involvement. As he said:

Ex-KP members and female managers who had worked for massage parlor houses sometimes have a partnership and operate massage parlors because they know how to make easy and big money. But you have to understand that they are older members who run a private business and have nothing to do with the KP organization.

Factions were at odds with one another, resulting in numerous acts of violence. As Tae-Ho described, "When Khwang-Soo (another faction leader) and his kids come here and disturb business (a nightclub and bar), I won't let them fight with my brothers and mess up my business here. What I do and all I need to do is just take care of Khwang-Soo, then the rest of them are also taken care of." He said, "That's the only way to avoid unnecessary group fighting or any other serious situation." Inter-gang violence used to be inevitable when business-extortion areas overlapped with the Korean Fuk Ching gang. Again, Tae-Ho described, "They (the Fuk Ching gang) went around the same stores where we collected money. There was fighting every week. Fuk Ching members easily got handguns through the Chinese Fuk Ching while we had to go here and there to get them. Only a couple of us had guns and those who didn't have guns carried knives, in case. But one day both leaders agreed to avoid any serious incident. After that, we ignored one another and collected money at the same stores." His account suggests that, in general, gang violence is considered unnecessary and that the leaders adopt various tactics to avoid group violence, although he did mention young, individual members engaged in fighting.

Since the major financial source of the gang, extortion, was not available, the Korean Power gang broke apart. Tae-Ho claims,

> That's the reason why many KP members left and the organization is hibernating. See, Oyaboong did not share the profits from his illegal enterprise with other members, and, at the same time, extortion became slow. Obviously, there were not good enough money-generating businesses out there for young KP members. They were sort of getting out of the KP and the group eventually died out.

This breakdown of the original Korean Power gang with the change of illegal opportunities available in the community resulted in a different pattern of group activities which still focused on money-generating businesses, while some old ex-gang members set up individual illegal businesses. Instead of collecting protection money, they established a partnership with Korean owners and shared the profits. One faction also developed their gang businesses such as street drug-selling and insurance fraud after extortion opportunities dried up. Some individual ex-gang members, as they got older and more experienced, actually ran businesses like massage parlors as a partnership with female managers.

Under the Influence of Chinese Gang Subculture

Compared to those in Palisades Park, a distinguishing characteristic of Korean youth groups in Flushing grows quite simply out of the fact that they are in close contact with the Chinese subculture in the community. Of the various aspects of Flushing's Korean youth groups in which a distinctive gang character is best preserved, the Korean- affiliated Chinese gang is the most conspicuous.

The reasons why Koreans join Chinese gangs vary. As seen earlier, those who had Korean gang experience indicate that following Korean custom was a great burden to them and that is the main reason they shifted to Chinese gangs. Others indicate multiple reasons. As a Green Dragon gang member says, "I think there are many kinds of attractiveness. They (Chinese gangs) were more financially secure and name-wise were recognized. In a sense, they have more to offer or they are out there recruiting more aggressively." But the reason most frequently mentioned was the friendship they had with Chinese gang members. A Mo Ming Pai member explains, "A lot of the friends I could relate to were Chinese in MMP. I am in MMP so I'm like hanging out with them because I can relate to them more because they are my friends, you know." Another Mo Ming Pai member provides the same explanation, "I have a few friends in it. They were my friends a long time ago through other friends, and schools, and hanging out, I guess. I started hanging out when I was thirteen and then I met people when I hung out. And then they end up joining MMP and I hang out with them." These statements reveal that young Koreans interact, cooperate, and associate with their Chinese peers, the major ethnicity group of the community, before they join the gangs. A Green Dragon member illustrates how the number of Korean members in Chinese gangs increased in the community:

> One joins the group and recruits as a friend and friend of friends to the group. When you see a gang, one way or another they know each other before they join the gang. It's not like they join individually. But most likely they join as a group. I'm talking about a week or a month difference in joining.

In addition to young Koreans having Chinese gang membership, certain characteristics of the Chinese gang subculture in the community may be considered in general as the primary locus of the passing on of Chinese gang subculture traits to the Korean-only gangs. This diffusion of Chinese gang subculture to Korean gangs may have to do with cohabitation in the same community where the knowledge and practice of Chinese gang traits are also communicated from individual to individual within the community, besides cultural sharing by the two ethnic groups. The effect is indeed very pronounced. For example, the Korean Power gang structure resembles the Chinese tong-affiliated gangs in the sense that businesspersons are involved. Their activities also have the similar pattern and path of Chinese gangs as Chin (1996) found in New York City's Chinatown gangs, which are well known for their activities in extortion, running illegal gambling places, and operating massage parlors. None of the Korean Power informants here indicated the direct influence of Chinese gang subculture. However, both mentioned that Korean groups in the community learn sufficient knowledge of Chinese gang activities to respond favorably to the image of Chinese gangs, saying that Chinese gangs are better organized and well established, which is a sign of the diffusion of Chinese gang subculture to young Korean people.

Hiding Gang Identification: No Name, No Dress Code, and No Tattoos

While conducting the study, I found it is often very difficult to distinguish between delinquent groups and gangs because gangs tend to hide their identification to outsiders. There are no specific dress codes, tattoos, or hand signs used as a means of group identification. Even many gang members that I interviewed denied their gang membership at the first meeting. For example, Tae-Ho initially went to great lengths to conceal his affiliation with the Korean Power gang. Moreover, Tae-Ho's faction does not use the name Korean Power. Interestingly, the meaning of the Mo Ming Pai gang is also interpreted as "no-name gang" in English. The police crackdown on Asian gangs affected not only their pattern of group activities but also their gang identification. As a Green Dragons gang member illustrates,

> The identity of the gang actually has been changed. A couple of years ago, a lot of group names were recognized, but also there were a lot of federal crackdowns and raids. Green Dragons was raided and high-up members were arrested. Same thing happened with Flying Dragons, Ghost Shadows, and Korean Power. A lot of gang members were prosecuted by federal and state authorities. They used to identify themselves by clothing and tattoos. It was recognizable what gang and what group you belonged to. But because a lot of

arrests have been made, they were wise enough to know that it's not quite smart if they have a group name..... A lot of these income-focused groups actually tried to dissociate themselves from group names even though at one time they might have had one. They might be active as a group or associated with a group name; these gentlemen might even identify themselves as Green Dragons, but not they go out in public. 'I'm Green Dragons, Green Dragons.' They won't advertise as much as before. You don't see much identification.

CHAPTER 6

The Delinquent Group: Joong and His Boys

As described in the preceding chapter, delinquent groups speak for themselves in terms of how they differ from gangs. In any given analysis, therefore, it requires great care to differentiate one from the other. To convey the idea of the delinquent group and its dynamics, the study selected a delinquent group and measured its group structure, process, and activities. The delinquent group also includes Fobbies, although some members are shared with the Twinkies. Group structure is measured by its size, average age of their members, and its leadership. Since these structural characteristics change as the group evolves, the analysis keeps pace with the group process which is measured through the life cycle of the group in terms of onset, persistence, and desistance. Group activities are measured by the level of delinquent activities such as violence and drug involvement.

THE DELINQUENT GROUP STRUCTURE

By every measure, the delinquent group, to which twelve members belonged, was, at least during the data collection period, the largest group of the three identified in Palisades Park, and perhaps the most active delinquent group in the neighborhood (Please see appendix E for the twelve members' profiles). Moreover, as I observed, members of the group, either the older boys or younger boys, were gathered primarily by Joong. The description of the group is basically made around Joong for the convenience of the data analysis, and the title of this chapter, "Joong and His Boys," also reflects this.

Size

The delinquent group had a total of twelve members at its maximum size between July 2000 and January 2001, during the data collection period. The immediate group began with three members, who started hanging out at the beginning of March 1999. Soon after, they started to associate with two young adults who were older than they were. Instead of "recruitment" of these two young adults, it would be a more accurate description to say that the younger boys were willing to associate with the young adults. The group then became five members beginning in June 1999. Although a couple of other boys were closely acquainted with the group through the billiard games, they did not see themselves as part of the group. As will be described in the group process, two events increased the number of group members dramatically. In February 2000, fighting brought five younger members into the group. Four months later, the group reached its maximum number of twelve members after the two youngest members were allowed to participate in a group party in July 2000.

After the group enjoyed its largest membership between July 2000 and January 2001, the group members somehow faded out quickly. By the time of completing the data collection, the size of the group had shrunk to six members, who were divided into three twosomes. Each twosome occasionally met another but there was no event that brought all six members together by the end of June 2001.

It also should be noted that after the size of the group became larger, the group had difficulty in scheduling meetings so that all members could participate; also, the members' interests changed as they grew up. This directly affected the activities they pursued and the length of time the group stayed together, as well as the cohesiveness among members.

Age

The group was structured along strict age lines. The mean age of the twelve members was 17.6, ranging from sixteen years old to twenty years old in June 2000. The two youngest boys were sixteen years old. Five members were seventeen years old. There was a clique of eighteen-year-olds within the group, consisting of three members. The oldest clique was composed of two young adults, age twenty. Usually cliques with the same age got together unless there was a whole group event.

Within the group, age is the basic component of the group structure and is an important criterion for judgment of its membership, relationship among members, and behavioral patterns. First, age is associated with entry into the group. For instance, when the youngest boys were fifteen, they were not able to have full membership although they were allowed to hang out with the group members occasionally. Second, age is significantly related to behavioral norm expectations among members. Regardless of grade in school or contribution to the group, older members always have a certain level of superiority to younger members. For example, younger members must not talk back to older members, and must use the term "Hyung" (Brother) as an expression of respect. If older members say something, what they say goes. Older members also feel obligated to look after younger members, and older members usually pay expenses (i.e. meals) for younger members without really expecting anything in return. As a result, this basic age rule leads younger members to follow older members' leadership. Third, age affects the types of offense pattern dramatically. Younger members tend to engage in violent acts while older members engage in non-violent activities. It should be noted that members in general, as they age, are less frequently engaged in violent activities compared to their behavior before they join the group.

Membership through Peer Network

The members connected with one another through three different social network processes: school, neighborhood and kinship. The largest pool of membership obviously began through the school setting. When the group size was at its maximum, nine members were attending one of two neighborhood high schools. Six members were attending Palisades Park High, while three were in Ridgefield. Another three members were dropouts from either one of the two schools. Individual members first created small companionships with the same age line in school. Then, this small age-subgroup as a unit joined in the group later.

Neighborhood networks played a key role in connecting members from two different schools. Four members were in this network. Two members established their friendship outside the school setting because of their parents' working relationship. The other two members met through gambling in the billiard club. While they frequently played gambling pool together, they developed a friendship when they realized they were the same age.

Six members out of twelve were linked through kinship as well. Four members were brothers and two were cousins. This suggests that a common kinship shares personal experiences and values, which results in an influence on individual member's group associations. It must be mentioned, however, that the brothers constantly engaged in conflict with each other. Most of time, the conflict started over a small matter. A member gave one example. "When my brother asks me to get soda or water, I say, if you want, go and get it yourself. Then, he's getting all overheated and says not to sass him back. Nothing important, but that's why we finally came to blows." Another member also complained about his younger brother, "He's so stupid sometime, like taking my car and stealing my money. He's my brother. But he's a stupid jerk, too." These statements reflect that the brothers did not show any strong level of intimacy. Therefore, brothers may be more likely to play an indirect role in membership instead of having a direct influence.

Gender

There were no female members in the group and no group of girls associated with the group. However, there were individual girls who were often seen with the group. Members used the terms either "girlfriend" or "gulrae (slut)" to describe girls who hang out with them. About half of the members were seeing somebody at any point during the data collection, although their girlfriends kept changing. These individual members often went out with their girlfriends. Members generally considered them "decent girls," as compared to girls who were labeled "gulrae". Many of their girlfriends had dropped out of school before or after they met members. Girlfriends were usually younger than members. It was rare to see a member bring his girlfriend to regular group hangout places. When their girlfriends were invited, it normally would be for a subgroup party or special occasion.

Unlike girlfriends, girls called by the term "gulrae" were more likely to be sexually promiscuous. These girls regularly hung out with members in recreational activities such as in a nightclub, billiard club, and Internet café, as the following conversation reveals:

KS: Is there any difference between a girl--you used the term 'gulrae'-- and your girlfriend?

Manho: It's about sex. If she is a gulrae, it's on the spot. Gulraes don't care about it. If she is my girlfriend and I really like her, then it took about a month to have a sex with her because I wanna save her.

KS: How do you know if she is gulrae?

Manho: We know that. Everyone knows who is gulrae or not. Rumor is serious among us. If rumor has it that a girl is a gulrae, she is the bottom of the pit. For example, if I had her and someone that I know had her, then she is gulrae. That's it. There might be some other stupid guys who don't know about the rumor who made friends with the girl. But, that's not happened with our guys.

KS: Does that mean the girls that I saw hanging out with your group are not gulraes?

Manho: Yes, Regina and Jennifer are gulraes

KS: How do you meet with them?

Manho: Regina worked in Dolche (Korean pub) where we used to go. I am not quite sure but Sungjin met Jennifer in a (Internet) chatting room and we found out she's gulrae.

KS: Do you feel O.K. hanging out with these girls?

Manho: No, I don't like them. Regina lives alone after she ran away from home. I know younger brothers sometimes have sex with her. I warned young brothers not to get in trouble because of the gulrae.

KS: Do you know any girl who got pregnant?

Manho: Yes. I know a gulrae who went to Chinatown and had an operation.

KS: Why Chinatown?

Manho: I don't know. All our guys know her

Although there is less time elapsed between the initiation of dates and entering into sexual relationship, in contrast to their girlfriends, members stereotyped girls with the label gulrae as promiscuous sex objects. There is also concern when a girl has multiple sex partners in the group, particularly with younger members. As Kangso expressed it, "Having sex with a girl by younger brothers would be practically incestuous." Whether it has to do with the label gulrae, older members who have a girlfriend personally tend to avoid taking their girlfriends to group situations especially after an affair or if their relationship becomes serious.

Leadership

The group does not have a clear leadership pattern and seems to function without one particular leader. If anything, older boys act as leaders in the group due to the age structure of the group. It should be noted when there were only two age-graded cliques (eighteen years and twenty years old), the two oldest members, Dongbin and Kangso, significantly influenced the activities of the group. After Joong brought younger members to the group, the group activity plans were made through the clique of the eighteen-year-old boys and the two twenty-year-olds. Members often allow them to make decisions on many entertainment activities. The following dialogue with Joong and Kunsun indicates a clique leadership:

KS: Who is considered as a leader in the group?

Kunsun: There is no leader in our group.

KS: O.K. then, is there anyone who often makes decisions about fighting or parties?

Joong: We all make decisions together.

Kunsun: In Korea, there must be only one Jjang in the school. Here, we are all Jjangdll (the plural form of Jjang in Korean). If we are walking on the street, we walk like we are Jjangdll. If any one of us has a problem with another group, we jump in all together.

KS: Was there any problem in-group decision-making? For example, you have a plan, but the others have a different plan.

Joong: Usually, we don't have that kind of problem.

Kunsun: Joong is somewhat stubborn…. extremely stubborn, right?

Joong:...

Kunsun: Let us say, he wants to do this, then he must do it. I am like, whatever they decide is all right with me. I really do not care.

Joong: Yes. It is more about stubbornness rather than leadership. They know my personality and they usually do what I want to do. If Manho really wants to do something, I usually make a deal. For example, we do what I want to do first, then we do what he wants.

KS: Do Kangso or Dongbin make any decisions for the group?

Joong: Yes they still do. However, they usually do not mind whatever we like to do with younger brothers, and they just join us.

KS: Do younger members share any group decision-making?

Joong: No. They listen to what I say. They're supposed to…

Despite a group of older members who made decisions on group activities, Joong's dominance over younger members was more powerful. It may have been due to either his "toughness" and physical prowess or the fact that he was the only older member who was taking courses with younger members in the school. In some cases of fighting, Joong asked all members to be a fighting force to back up younger member(s) if he believed the size of the group mattered in the fighting. In the case of a party, he acts as a representative of the older members and allows the younger boys to smoke and drink as well as to share drugs in front of older members. There also existed situations where younger members expected Joong to engage in or lead the group when they were having trouble with adult figures in a school setting or in the Korean community, as will be described later concerning his reaction to a schoolteacher.

Even though the group structure had not been clear-cut, it must be remembered that the group was formed and enlarged around him. In addition, his role in the group and his influence on the group appears to have made him a natural leader, though without any title or acknowledgement.

THE DELINQUENT GROUP PROCESS

To analyze the group process, I divided it into three different stages: onset, persistence, and desistance. The onset stage explains the emergence of the group with main causal factors such as negative labeling attached to the members, fun seeking, and interpersonal violence. The persistence stage identifies three entertainment sources which bring members together and drive the group as a whole, continuously, to evolve. The desistance stage discusses disassociation of group members from the group and breakdown of the group.

Onset

The delinquent group was initially formed out of two schoolboys' close friendship. They knew each other as a matter of course in the school where they were labeled as troublemakers. It is interesting to note that this school experience, in turn, made them seek out each other. Joong explained, "All Korean students know one another in school. But, I know Manho better because he's tough. Well, I guess, I am tough, too (laugh). I like him 'cause he got the heart like me." Joong also described some schoolteachers as racists who were already ascribing the label of deviant to him. He recalled one event when a schoolteacher berated them, "You Koreans! What are you guys doing back there all the time?" Instead of simply explaining to the teacher what they were doing, Joong had to stand up against the schoolteacher because the younger boys' eyes were on him. He goes on, "Actually, it's none of his fucking business, you know. I don't remember what I said to him but it went really bad. I got out-school suspension because of it. I hate him. He's a piece of shit and a dumb-ass racist. Some other teachers are, too. They just don't like us because we are Koreans." His label as a troublemaker and other school experiences made other school colleagues believe the Koreans to be tough and to treat them accordingly. At this time period, they began to adjust to the label imposed on them. In addition, for their own sake, they adopted this popular, stereotyped "toughness or troublemaking" label for comfort and affiliation. Manho recalls the day Joong got his suspension. "I went to his house after school. And, we...like...we cursed schoolteachers and principals pretty much all day, you know." Since then the two boys curse in Korean when the teacher passes by, pretending that they are talking to each other.

This intimate two-boy group met a same-age boy, who was also being labeled "tough," though attending a different school, through the neighborhood network in the Korean community. All three were of the same age although Joong was one grade below the other two boys. Joong explains how they got together in the following dialog:

KS: How did you first meet Kunsun?

Joong: When I think about the day we first met, it's a little weird 'cause Manho and Kunsun were having noodles in my apartment (Joong let Manho know where his apartment key was after Manho's dropout in October 1998. Later he also told me the key was under the doormat and allowed me to stay when no one would be there). They knew each other because their moms are friends. Actually, Manho's mom works for Kunsun' mom's nail salon. But, I kinda knew him 'cause he was a Jjang (No. 1 in fighting) in Ridgefield High School.

KS: How do you know he's Jjang?

Joong: It's small stuff, but when we got together, talking about who's doing what in Ridgefield High (School), Fort Lee High, and Leonia. Even they're talking about what's going on in Flushing, (New York).

KS: Did you like him when you first saw him?

Joong: It's just like, we just liked each other. We smoked and drank all night long. Then, we're pretty much together. When I cut class, I ask him to cut class, too. We do pretty much everything together and we became best friends.

The labeling and reaction to it does not appear so uniform to other members, particularly to the younger boys who joined the group about one year later. Although there was still deviation from their responses, when they were asked how they liked school, many younger boys responded positively. As Saemin reveals, he ignored negative experiences and reinforced positive ones. "Sometimes, I feel people are talking something behind my back, but I never care 'cause there is nothing I can do about my look and my language." He continues, "Personally, I don't like it (school), but there is always encouragement and someone who says 'Good work! Well done!' I didn't get that kind of attention from any of my teachers in Korea. When you hear this, you just want to keep moving on." His impression about schoolteachers' encouragement was not coincidence; it was due to his excellence in math and science. The following conversation is another good example of the young boys' school experience:

Namsoo: I like school. Sometimes, there is lots of pressure. But, in school, you can see many friends and have fun.

KS: Can you describe something more about schools, perhaps related to teachers?

Namsoo: They don't care as long as you shut up. Some say they look down on Korean students but I don't feel anything like that personally.

KS: Have you ever been in suspension or detention?

Namsoo: No, oh...no. I never got suspension or inside detention.

KS: How do you like your classes?

Namsoo: Not the best, but I guess I'm doing O.K. at school and trying to be a good student. I am not interested in learning but believe if I stick to the school, I'll get further education.

Another boy says that he used to have a bad reputation among schoolteachers. However, he tried to study hard because of his parents' concern about his academic success. In addition, some teachers changed their attitudes toward him. "They are really nice to me now. It's hard to do make-believe things like that but you know I feel like I have to."

When they are asked why they got into the group, most of the members mentioned greater ease of adjustment and a sense of belonging. These statements are particularly interesting for in-group analysis that makes a sharp difference between members who initially form a group and those who associate with the group. Younger members generally show an uneasy feeling toward not only other ethnic groups, but also other Korean peer groups. For instance, Majoong explained the reason why he could not mingle with other Korean students:

Some Korean kids, they're talking about what universities and colleges they apply to or think of visiting them with their parents. Otherwise, what kind of summer job they would get, you know. I'm getting sick of it. Then, I just happened to be hanging out with Joong "Hyung" (brother) and other Hyungdle" (brothers).

In addition, Eugene, who also described an uneasy feeling when he was with other ethnic groups, notes, "We're talking a lot of baseball. I'm a great fan of the Yankees and most of them are, too. But, if you'd talk about a Korean player, by the way, you know Chan Ho Park in LA Dodgers, right, some of them don't know him or they'd say he's no good. I'd ask them why, and they'd say 'cause he won't make it, you think he's the greatest player. You know, there's just something in there, a feeling you get when you're there but can't put into words." As a result, "With them (his group members), it's fun and I won't get that kind of strange feeling or be out of place."

The other motive of full participation in the group that the younger members frequently mentioned was "having fun." Like Eugene's description, they see the "fun" quality can only be obtained through membership. As Saemin adds, "I wanna be like them. I wanna go to parties and stay out all night, and I wanna be cool, you know. They're cool and seem always to be having fun. I wanna be a part of it, and be cool."

There was indirect sibling influence as well. For example, Sungjin was motivated to join the group after observing the fun part of the group life through his brother, Kunsun, although Sungjin had noticed and was concerned about changes in Kunsun' behavioral pattern after his association with the group members. As he describes it, "He is not like that. He just keep(s) going out with them (and) being late. It's like he's not my brother. There was a huge change in him." However, when he began to see group members and occasionally join group activities, he wanted to join the group himself. As the following conversation indicates, indirect sibling influence played a role in his willingness to join the group.

KS: Why didn't you like the way your brother changed?

Sungjin: 'Cause I thought he would run away from home again.

KS: If I remember correctly, your brother ran away a couple of times.

Sungjin: He did it two times. Then, Mom paid more attention to him. That's how he gets his BMW and all the new stuff. I was kinda jealous of him but, uh, I tried to understand, 'cause I saw my mom crying every night and looking for him.

KS: I want to be myself clear here because you said you didn't like how your brother changed. Then, how did it happen that you joined your brother's group?

Sungjin: I just wanna hang out with them

KS: There must be some reasons why you wanted to?

Sungjin: I don't know. It's like ...you see, they (were) having a party in the house. It's completely different. It's a real party. Then, they go out again to some place. At this time, they won't let me go with them because my brother always says I'm too young, you know.

KS: Is your mom around during the party?

Sungjin: (chuckling) You kiddin' me? No.

Fun activities, particularly parties, go on in a couple of members' houses when their parents are not present. Most of the time, Joong and Dongbin brothers' apartment is a base of party operations, simply because of the absence of parents. Sungjin finally became a member with his friend, Saemin, through a party during summer break 2000. Since there was no group initiation for new members, he was drunk,-- like all the other members, smoked marijuana, and engaged in sexual intercourse with a girl after the party. Interestingly, the idea of fun often carries with it secondary deviant behaviors such as drinking alcohol, taking drugs, and engaging in sex.

Although no one mentions a sense of empowerment or status as a reason for joining the group, it must be mentioned here by looking at a fighting event involving the younger boys. Refer to the attachment of the individual member description: although Joong and four boys, Namsoo, Hyunsoo, Majoong, and Eugene, are acquainted with one another, their association was limited to a school setting until Dojung's sudden appearance and his aggressive behavior toward the Korean students, which results in fighting and a new matter of concern among the Korean students.   Although it is unknown how Dojung can be enrolled in a public school, he beat up two Korean students in his first school week and set up another fight with Namsoo. Although fighting did not break out between them, due to Joong's intervention, all of them eventually joined the group because of the event.   Dojung's affiliation with the group can be understood, on the one hand as self-labeling "toughness," on the other hand as attaining status in his new school setting. As he describes it, "I was a 'Jjang' and I don't see why I can't be the 'Jjang' here."   Instead of an ongoing conflict with the Korean students, he decided to subordinate himself to Joong as an expression of respect for older people, according to Korean culture, and became a member of the group, which led him to secure his status in the new environment.

With minimum contact with younger boys in the school and community contexts, the group was kept exclusively to five older boys. Thus, for Namsoo and the other boys, the fighting provided an opportunity to open the gate of the group, which was closed to them before, and to attain a sense of empowerment due to their attachment to Joong, which in turn helped them maintain the informal peer social order threatened by Dojung. It seems clearly to indicate that deviant labeling and reaction to it is an important part of the group formation, while the attainment of a sense of power or maintenance of informal peer social order is important for the group association of younger boys.

Persistence

As has been discussed so far, the group was initially formed by the reaction to labeling attached to them and then became larger due to an event where a new student, Dojung, threatened the informal peer order in the school.   Nonetheless, the factors that produced the delinquent group and new members for the group were not sufficient for group sustenance and the creation of delinquent group behaviors. It should be noted that members as a whole somehow pull together through entertainment activities, which often involve delinquent behaviors. When individual members were asked their daily activities, a majority of them responded with hanging out, watching videos, or participating other routine activities. However, when the members were asked their group activities, their answers shifted dramatically to entertainment activities. These group activities are also limited to specific places that were, in fact, observed socially and physically during the data collection period. Out of many, let me take you on a brief tour of three major hangout places: Billiard Club, PC Bang (Internet Café), and Nightclub or Pub.

Billiard Club

Members of the group usually get together in the "Star" billiard club around midnight on weekends during the school session. The time of gathering becomes earlier during the summer break. My social and physical observation of the site normally began about 11 pm before the parking lot was full. The club is a two-story building with two entrances. It is open twenty-four hours a day, seven days a week. On any typical weekend of my study, the first floor at this billiard club is full of young people more than half of whom are non-Asian, mostly whites. At any moment on the first floor, some youths are playing arcade games or the jukebox located on the right-hand side of the first-floor entrance; some are sitting on chairs chatting with one another, some are waiting for their turn at a pocket ball game while observing the opposing player's shot. Loud music is turned on, and cigarette smoke fills the first floor. Non-smokers never could stay long inside because of the pervasive cigarette smoke.

On the second floor, there are fourteen billiard tables and none of them has pockets. Before 11 pm on weekends, these tables are occupied and played by Koreans. During the entire data collection period, I never saw any non-Asians play a game of pool on this floor. Ordinarily, the scene here is quite different. No loud music is heard. Nonetheless, more than fifty people including bystanders make the floor look very busy and dense during the weekends. All clients on this floor are served with either free coffee or soda. People can have instant noodles, seaweed and rice, or other instant food by paying for it. Typically, three billiard tables near the cashier's table are assigned for gambling games such as nine balls or three-cushion game. Those who play at gambling game look much more serious.

Kangso and Dongbin usually play a gambling game with other young adults. Unlike other members, they come here almost every day and the duration of their play is longer than other members'. "Sometimes I played the game for twelve hours straight and when it's 7 o'clock in the morning, I just go to work without any sleep," Dongbin said. Because of his addiction to gambling, he actually suffered from sleep deprivation and was often unable to perform his duties at work, which caused him to be fired four times within one year. Although I observed him to be an advanced player, he lost $600 playing twelve games in succession. All the players seemed to be uninterested in talking to one another. During the gambling activity, players simply sit back and wait for their turn while watching the opposing player's shot. Sometimes, players give felicitations for a beautiful shot with a nod of the head but not to the player who made such a shot. All you can hear for four or five hours is, "I had no luck today," "Coffee, please" in the middle of the game, or "Let's cut it off today" at the end.

Joong and Manho sometimes join the gambling but normally play an ordinary pool game with Kunsun or the other younger boys. When there is a match between two members or two groups, competition for victory is often intense. As Joong said: "Most of the time, it's O.K. But when I lost because I was not thinking, and if any of the boys acts a little annoyed after the game, I am really steamed." The billiard game itself was a great topic for the younger boys soon after they began to learn how to play. They talked about a game that they lost in their last match due to a missed possible shot. In addition, they all seemed to agree that it was the shots they could cost them the games. As Saemin told me, "It's really fun to play a pool game. We're all crazy about it and talk about it like all day long." When I asked what exactly they talked about the game, he continued, "It's…about your stance, head position, stroke…uh…consistent line-up of cue ball to object ball, stuff like that." It is safe to say that the billiard club is the most active hangout place, and pool games and gambling there become the group's core activity.

PC Bang (Personal Computer Cafe)

The daily concern of young members of the group is with a source of amusement. If the billiard club is their weekend night attraction, PC Bang is another favorite place of the group gathering after school for entertainment from Monday to Friday. There are three PC Bangs on Broad Street, outfitted with the high-speed Internet connections that make interactive games crackle. Like the billiard club, they are open twenty-four hours, but charge just $1 an hour to use a computer, compared to $12 an hour to play a pool game; they are also well stocked with sausages, potato wafers, and instant noodles. Each PC Bang has around fifteen to twenty desktop computers.

Many young people play the "Starcraft"[7] online game. Since the Starcraft online game allows for up to eight players over networks around the world, younger members of the group share the resources for the game and often play as a team. In Starcraft, gamers playing military leaders of each of three different species known as Terran, Protoss, and Zerg, fight one another to survive on the edge of the galaxy by gaining control of the resources. The game is attractive and addictive because of its complex feudal environment, which hooks players after they invest days or weeks building up the strength of their online characters. Although it is an online game, they take it seriously. When their virtual characters are destroyed, the result can bring on real life violence among gamers. As Majoong describes an incident, "We (were) really steamed up and we found him in (a PC Bang) Fort Lee. We just beat him real bad." He continues "This guy already used cloaked Ghosts to lockdown my Battle Cruisers whenever I built lots of Battle Cruisers to attack his town. (He) then use(d) Stim Packed Marines, Wraiths, and then Goliaths to finish mine off. EMP's also (used) to knock out Yamato cannons on my Cruisers." Although he explained with great seriousness what had happened in cyber space, he spoke to me strange, nearly foreign language.

In PC Bangs, young people also engage in video chatting since all the computers have cameras on them. Young members of the group usually make good conversation and friends via online chatting. However, the main purpose of the video chatting to loaf while searching for Korean females either in Korea or in the United States. In chatting, they spending their time telling filthy stories, exchanging cyber information, or asking a girl out if she lives in New York City or New Jersey. One night in a PC Bang, I was having instant noodles, and talking with Joong and his brother Dongbin, when Sungjin's shout of

---

[7] In the game, the gamer acts as a military leader for three different species, the gamer must gather the resources he or she needs to train, expand his or her forces, and lead them to victory. Thirty unique missions challenge the gamer across three different campaigns as he or she controls the fate of the galaxy.

delight shook the PC Bang. We approached his computer, and there was a girl taking off her clothes on the screen. After seeing the girl waving her hand to the screen, Dongbin gibed, "She is a porno." To this, Sungjin asserted, "No, she is not. I was talking to her for two hours. She is real and I don't pay anything." This kind of dialogue is rare. Nonetheless, individual members often obtain porno website information through chatting, and regular visits to such websites that have exceedingly demoralizing contexts are common practice.

Until Manho was hired on the night shift in a PC Bang, members did not have one specific PC bang for their gathering. They even moved from one PC Bang to another a couple of times in a day to kill time or find other members, which was possible for them because all three PC Bangs were within five minutes' walking distance on Broad Street. When Manho could not work seven days, he introduced Joong and Kunsun to the owner of the PC Bang, and the three of them were working there in January 2000. Since the owner stopped by only once a day to collect money, the site was worry-free from adults. The members' gatherings also dramatically shifted from Joong's house to the PC Bang. Members enjoyed their privileges when they used computers, without any charge. This is possible when the main computer that is connected to all the computers individually on the floor is not turned on so that the time being used for that computer does not count. When all the clients are gone by early morning, it often turns into a party place for the group.

Nightclub or Pub

Although the PC Bang became one of the favorite party places, along with Joong's house or other members' houses when no parents were present, the best time for the group amusement was through parties in nightclubs or Korean pubs where there was no ID check. There are always some kinds of parties all year long, including birthday parties for members, their girl friends or a member's friend, summer break, graduation parties, and Christmas parties. These parties are normally planned with places to go and amounts of money to collect. Nonetheless, the party itself is not well organized. For example, the group usually sets up a meeting place in front of Rodeo Plaza on Broad Street. However, it takes almost two or three hours to get everyone together. While waiting for members who are late, some go to have a quick bite in local restaurants. Some want to play online games in PC

Bangs. Some go inside the coffee shop in the Rodeo Plaza building. Almost two hours after the meeting time, members keep calling each other by cellular phones, asking where and who they are with, until they figure it out that all the members are somewhere on Broad Street. Then, they all get together in front of Rodeo Plaza.

The places for the parties and the member dues are varied. If they decide to go to Korean pubs, females (members' girlfriends) do not pay any fees but males pay around $100 due to their heavy drinking. If they have a party at a member's house, the cost is much less, but usually they go to a Karaoke bar after celebrating the party at home. Thus, it costs around $50 or $60 for males to cover the expenses of girls, if any. The cost is again varied depending on how much drinking they have at the Karaoke. When they want to go to nightclubs, the cost is very high, and females have to pay around $100. On Friday night, February 9, 2001, I was invited to Joong's birthday party. Since all the members had already gotten together to celebrate his real birthday party the previous Tuesday in Joong's house, it would be his second birthday party. The birthday party rule was applied to me, too. Except for the birthday person, males paid $150 and females $100 for the party. However, boyfriends paid dues for their girlfriends. A total of eleven people got together; six members of the group, four of their girlfriends, and me. As my observation note indicates from the arrival to leaving the nightclub:

> It was a slightly cold Friday night around 9 pm by the time we arrived by three different call taxis. In front of the nightclub, two guards stood and checked IDs for each person. There was a little trouble with IDs but they let us go into the club after frisking us. It is unknown what they were looking for exactly (probably weapons, not drugs). Excitement started the minute members walked through the front door of the Korean nightclub in Manhattan. The colorful changing walls, the illuminated bar and the fiber optics were all a part of the show, which created the mood and the ambience in the club. Loud techno music[8] captivated and enthralled young members and kept them coming out to the dance floor.

---

[8] A type of electronic dance music played in the club where disk jockeys manipulate hard-to-find music, sometimes working with just a set of beats and samples, into a tapestry of mind-bending music.

The floor was hot and full of young people dancing. A description that is more accurate would be that there was no individual space on the floor. One's skin had to contact others' skin in order to move inside of the club. No one cared about being that close with others. People danced and talked to each other with a bottle of water in their hands. No one could make any communication with others unless one spoke into the other's ear. People were everywhere in the club. They were standing, smoking, drinking, talking, and dancing any place if there was a space.

A waiter guided us to tables. Each table had a basic minimum charge. It started from $300 for up to four persons. We were guided into one large round table with a minimum of $800 for the eleven of us. All we got were a bottle of beer per person, two snack side dishes and two fruit plates for the whole table. Our bill went up almost $1,000 due to additional orders, which were ten bottles of water and one more side dish without including tips. Upon sitting on the sofas, Kunsun, Joong, Dongbin, and Kangso took Ecstasy. A minute later, Kangso and Kunsun' girl friends shared an Ecstasy and took it. No one asked what they were taking. It seemed so natural. Two other girls, Joong's and Eugene's girlfriends, went to the bathroom and came back. Although I could not tell whether they took Ecstasy or not, all four girls went to the floor and started dancing with lighting toys that were turning around with light and making a strange (fantastic?) mood in the dark. The rest of us followed the girls. The techno music shook the entire club and I was feeling my heart beat with the tempo of the music.

When we came outside of the nightclub, it was about 2:10 am. There was a police patrol car parked in front of the building. Police officers inside of the car watched us coming out. There was no particular incident between the police and us. They seemed to know exactly what we were doing inside the club. Kangso, Kunsun and their girlfriends went to Video Bang (room)[9] in Manhattan. The rest of us came back to New Jersey and went to play a pool game until almost 5:00 am.

Since there are many parties and costs are relatively high, members were asked how they got the money. In their statements about their financial sources for the group activities, all members, with a variation, relied on their parents regardless of their parents' economic status. Older members who are working but lack funds for group activities ask their parents for money and promise they will pay it back when they get a salary,. Younger members usually get pocket money ranging from $400 to $1000 per month from their parents. If they run out of money by the end of month, they usually use their monthly tuition meant for private educational institutions. In the case of Hyunsoo and Namsoo, because their parents use personal checks for tuition, they get their money by lying to their parents, telling them that they need to buy educational materials. It is worth mentioning that when three or four members get together for their entertainment, one member usually pays all the expenses, saying, "I will shoot tonight." Due to younger members' excuse of educational expenses, they get their money more easily than older members. Nevertheless, an older member with two or three younger member covers expenses for younger members.

In general, there appears to be a social pattern for the group to thrive through recreational activities, which often induce various deviant behaviors and increase frequency and duration of group association for members. This pattern of maintaining group persistence establishes solidification among group members as well. However, it does not mean the group itself creates the motives for an individual member to commit delinquent behaviors. It seems likely, from the general nature of the delinquent group activities, when the group interacts with particular places and environments, individual members significantly gravitate toward delinquent behaviors as a whole.

---

[9] Korean Video Store where clients pick up their own video and watch it in a small room where members usually engage in sexual intercourse with their girl friends

Desistance

The recreational group activities maintained by group persistence lasted for less than one year. Although a great deal of hanging out in twosomes or threesomes still existed, the group activities became less and members began to dissociate, especially with the loss of their favorite place, the PC Bang. The town regulation that was passed in 1997 and carried heavy penalties for the violation of store operating time had a major influence on group disintegration. The regulation called for mandatory closing for PC Bangs after 10 p.m. under the general store category. The town started to enforce the regulation in the fall of 1999. After four consecutive $500 fines, the PC Bang closed down in January 2001. Three members lost their jobs and other members lost their privilege of free or discounted computer use. After an active search for a new job, Manho found a night shift job from 7 pm to 7 am for seven days a week except Tuesdays at Manhattan's Deli Store, which made it impossible for him to be hanging out with members. A couple of months later, another PC Bang also discontinued its business. Since there was only one PC Bang left, members had to wait for a longer time for their computer turn. Moreover, it has been the least attractive to members because of its location on the third floor of the Rodeo Plaza. Thus, the shutdown of the PC Bangs dissolved one of the individual members' main ties with the group.

Along with less frequent daily activities, certain things happened to individual members that aggravated disaffiliation from the group. Hyunsoo and Namsoo were found out by their parents in their absences from the private educational institute when Namsoo's mother brought a snack to the institute. Since their parents now regularly check their attendance with teachers, they are no longer able to hang out with members as often as before. Their best friends, Majoong and Eugene, were hanging around on Broad Street, but the duration of time spent was not as long as before.

On Saturday, March 10, 2001, all members get together to bid farewell to Kangso, who was joining the U.S. army. Although his enlistment was surprising news to members, it was a result of his constant hope of changing his unhappy life situation. As he once said about his drug use:

I started it when I was in the 8th grade but I am getting scared
to take them. Sometimes I felt so chilly and horrified. The
other day I felt like I'm going to die. You don't know the fear
that really scares you and want to get rid of it but you can't.
Then, I started to see ghosts… real ghosts. When I am home
alone, I felt like, I was stifling. I took trips (taking LSD) but I
was again in a giant box and no exit in it. I ask myself so
many times, why I'm here and what I'm doing here. I just
want to be gone anywhere, somewhere people don't know
about me…and I will be gone one day.

While in training, Kangso made two phone calls to Dongbin, whom I
saw couple of times in the billiard club but who appeared to be
completely disengaged from the younger boys after Kangso's farewell
party. He was hired by a billiard club and indulged in gambling with
adults.

Dojung also became completely dissociated from the group
because of his return to Korea in June 2001. Like Kangso's enlistment,
the group members expected Dojung would go back to Korea since he
had talked about it a couple of times. He and his mother had much
difficulty in adjusting to the new environment in the United States.
When we sat in a coffee shop about a week before he left, joy and grief
alternated in his breast. He said,

It's bittersweet. When I think about my friends here, I'm
feeling a little sad, but I am really excited about going back to
Korea. After my father passed away, we came with great
expectation to America to change our life. We thought the
living situation would be getting better at the beginning but it
was not. Actually, it was getting worse as time went along.

Sungjin and Saemin were the only members who actively hung out
as usual by the end of the data collection period. The time they spent
with the group dramatically shifted to their friends outside the group. It
seems that they formed another delinquent group, which is more
fighting-oriented. Saemin described, when he was asked about the
group activities, "It's hard to point it out but things changed and we
changed. It used to be everything's O.K. if it is fun. Now, brothers ask
if I am still going to that same place. They're different now."

This statement of group disintegration has to do with Joong and Kunsun. They decided to go to a community college. Kunsun in particular was ready to study again one year after since his high school graduation. Since then, they had talked more about tuition and their math placement test. Although they hang out with younger boys on a couple of occasions, they spend more time with their new girlfriends. As Joong said, "I'm really fed up with the same place crowded with young kids." His interests have changed since his high school graduation.

By the end of June, 2001, it was hard to see more than four members on the street. Their activities were also very few, which produced a reduction of delinquent involvement. Except for three members, Kangso, Dongbin, and Dojung, all other members' dissociation with the group was gradual and for various reasons. Commitment to or preparedness for education played a pivotal role in the dissociation process for some members.

THE DELINQUENT GROUP ACTIVITIES

As described in the section on group persistence, members construct their own patterns of delinquent behaviors in participating in group recreational activities. Consequently, the group, as a whole, developed a delinquent group action pattern, depending on opportunity structure in deviant places and instigation in a group context. Throughout group hangouts and delinquent experiences, each member created a conception of self as a group being and behaved according to the anticipated role of his actions. Two common forms of delinquent behaviors are drug use and fighting but they are not limited to such delinquent acts as gambling, mugging school-age youths, runaway from home, and sexual intercourse.

Drug Abuse

Alcohol

Members consumed alcohol on a regular basis. In a question on frequency of alcohol consumption, three members answered that they drank two or three times per week. Others responded that they drank at least once a week or every two weeks. In general, older members drank more often than younger members. When they were asked about quantity of alcohol consumption, binge drinking was identified as a common practice among group members. The binge drinking experience was determined by the quantity of alcohol consumed on any one drinking occasion. Although they did not specify brand names and sizes of bottles and glasses used for drinking, members generally responded that when they got together each member drank until he had consumed more than four cans of beer or one bottle of Soju (Korean brand alcohol) or half a bottle of whiskey.

Drinking locations varied from their own homes to restaurants to pubs. When younger members only got together, their own home or individual members' houses were the main places where they drank alcohol. However, when they were able to gain entry to licensed premises with older members, they usually went to local Korean restaurants or pubs. As indicated earlier, nightclubs were another favorite drinking location to celebrate special occasions such as birthdays or graduation. Many times, these places do not verify personal identification if some members are older-looking.

The main reason for drinking was their leisure time socializing with members. No one reported drinking alcohol when they were alone. Some members also mentioned they liked being drunk, which they believe ties them to one another. Nevertheless, the real problem is using a combination of drugs that include alcohol and at least one other drug such as marijuana and Ecstasy. Older members also had the experience of driving while intoxicated. Almost all members experienced sexual intercourse after they were drunk. A member, Joong, reported he had a run-in with police due to excessive drinking.

Other Illegal Substances

Aside from alcohol, marijuana was the most popular drug among members, followed by Ecstasy, LSD, and crack cocaine. No one reported ever trying heroin. The popularity of marijuana and Ecstasy has to do with accessibility and availability. Members can get marijuana even at school. Eugene said, "Marijuana is always available and I buy from friends I knew in school." The friends he mentioned were not Korean students. He added, "White guys sold them for money. They're not really dealers. The guy I know sells everything....Es, Ks, LSD, marijuana. My guess is he's sort of a friend of a friend who is a big dealer." Members also get drugs in Manhattan.

Kangso said, "I get them right off the (George Washington) bridge--there are dealers on the street." Kangso is the one who usually distributes drugs to members. For instance, Manho said, "Brother Kangso offers us some for free if he's got any to spare. Sometimes, if I ask him to get some for me, I usually get it a couple of days later. Then, I pay him back what he spent." Later, he and Kangso drove together to spots in Manhattan where African Americans sell drugs. Although Ecstasy pills can be obtained on the street or from school friends, members in general say they get them from the door staff or dealers in clubs.

Members had mixed emotions after they took drugs. All nine members who ever tried marijuana reported they felt relaxed and happy. Only one member mentioned he got a headache after the effects wore off. Reponses to Ecstasy were also positive. Seven members who had tried Ecstasy reported they felt energetic and friendly. They all took marijuana as well. However, they do not take both drugs at the same time. Their usual combination is either drinking and smoking marijuana or taking Ecstasy and drinking. Members took Ecstasy before they entered the club or inside the club. As Kunsun said,

> When we had dull (smoking marijuana), it's (in) someone's backyard and it's (marijuana) being passed around you know. But it's different when you're in the club. It is more about the atmosphere in the club that makes you try it. No one asks you to try it. You just feel like you have to try it if you wanna have fun.

The quantity of Ecstasy consumed varied. Six members reported taking only one pill for a night. Among them, some took half first and another half later. Others ingested one pill before or after entering a club. Manho is considered a heavy Ecstasy user. He usually took one and a half or two pills although he reported a maximum of three pills per night. Manho is also one of two members who tried LSD and crack cocaine with Kangso. Unlike other drugs, their experience of LSD and crack cocaine was unpleasant. They reported they were scared, anxious, and paranoid.

Like alcohol consumption, members usually tried drugs when they were in a group context, although Kangso and Manho had experiences taking them when they were alone. Since not a single member reported selling drugs for profit, drug use among members can be understood as a recreational purpose in a group context. Thus, the group recreational context is the most important factor that causes members to take drugs, in addition to easy access to drugs and other various effects they felt. Although some members were aggressive to non-members when they were drunk, members seemed to be at great ease when they took drugs. It is safe to say that there is no direct relationship between violence and drugs among the delinquent group members in general.

Violence

Fighting

The most common form of fighting is one-on-one fighting without weapons. Recall from the early discussion, setting up one-on-one fighting between Dojung and Namsoo eventually provided an opportunity for young boys to affiliate with the group when Joong intervened. Although this event had a different meaning compared to the one after they joined the group, the process of one-on-one fighting is similar. As Sungjin explained,

> We set up time and place with rival guys. All members go together but only two guys (one from our group and the other from a rival group) actually fight until one is down. That's it. We call (older) brothers sometimes when we do not trust the other guys or in case the guy may use weapons. Both sides understand nobody is going to jump in a fight.

In most one-on-one fighting, any one member can fight against another from the group. Dojung is usually one who volunteered for one-on-one fighting for the group. He said, "I fought a lot in Korea. I fought often because I fought until I won. The more you are experienced in fighting, the better you know how to fight." When he was asked why he fought, he replied, "Brothers here don't know how to fight. I don't want to see any of my brothers down." He also admitted that he was scared each time he engaged in one-on-one fighting. Initially, it seems that he wanted to act out aggressively to convince himself or group members of his fighting ability so that he could secure his status in the group. However, his role in the group somehow situated him to fight although he didn't want to.

There are minimal rules for the fight between two members of opposing groups, such as no interference from anybody in the group and no use of weapons. When these rules are broken, it becomes fighting between two groups. Saemin recalled the fighting over a girlfriend of his friend,

> I had to fight because a guy in Old Tappan insulted my friend's girlfriend. We both agreed to meet in a town park of Old Tappan. About fifteen or sixteen of my friends (including all younger members but without older members) rode about forty minutes to fight. When we got there, he was with about twelve Twinkies. I was really ready to fight. I pushed him. But, like all other Twinkies, he said 'Yo, we don't wanna do this.' I didn't give a shit and I started beating him. Then, the guys jumped in and my friends backed up. But we had to run away because they were backed up with another ten or more White friends.

Although fights between two groups are rare, I personally observed the group fighting in the parking lot of a billiard club. As a field observation note described, it was one Sunday early in the morning.

> The time got to be around 2:50 am. There was a big birthday party in Manhattan. About ten young people came in and they seemed to be drunk. Some of them kept saying "F" words and expressed themselves about tiredness. Except Dojung and Joong, members wanted to go home. Joong told them he would leave soon and asked Manho to give him a call tomorrow.

> However, a minute after they left, something was going wrong. A girl came up to Joong and Dojung with fear and worry. She took Joong to the other side of the hall. They talked about something seriously. Then, Joong came back and asked Dojung to hurry to leave. He informed me there was an argument between guys from New York and Kunsun (from New Jersey). A couple of young people playing billiard games followed them. For a moment, I hesitated but went after them.

There were about twenty young people in the parking lot outside the billiard club (although I wrote about twenty, It must have been more than thirty people because Joong told me people from New Jersey themselves were about twenty). The atmosphere itself was very scary. It was even difficult to distinguish who came from either New York or New Jersey. Three people were arguing and the rest of the young people stood around them. Because the parking lot was full of cars, three people arguing actually stood between two parked cars. The rest of the people surrounded the two cars. Less than a minute after I was on the spot, a young guy punched the other with a fist. All of sudden, the place became chaos. They were kicking, hitting, and shouting at one another in the dark. Some fell down on the ground, some were wrestling, some were fighting on the car, and many were bleeding.

A security guard came up and tried to break it up. But he seemed scared, too, and went back to the club. The fighting continued. There was a young person from New York brought to my attention during the fighting. He was small but had strong muscles like heavyweight boxer. He dealt with a couple of people at one time. He was hit, but he fought like a tank and he was fast. After another one or two minutes after the security guard got into the club, the manager and a person whose age was between thirty-five and forty with a billiard stick in his hand came out and shouted, "Stop" in Korean while swinging the stick. All this happened within about five minutes. People from both groups seemed to know him. He ordered the young people from New York to get in the car and get out of the place. The youth who fought well tried to explain what happened to him. However, he hit the youth with his stick real hard and ordered again for them to leave. They left.

After the break up of the fighting, I came to Joong and asked whether he was O.K. He was not listening to me and was worried about what would happen in the near future. He said to Kunsun, "They will come back."

The main reason for fighting almost invariably began with trivial personal matters such as staring, insults, and rumors. However, these myriad details are often considered signs of disrespect, which can result in individual fighting and then lead to group fighting. For example, the fighting Saemin described earlier was originally due to the insults to a girlfriend of his friend. It looks as if the insult itself had nothing to do with him. However, insults to friends or significant others of his or his friend brings him disrespect or takes on a much deeper meaning, such as a challenge to him or to his group as a whole. When I met Kunsun after the fighting, he explained how the fighting was started,

> That night, I met some guys from New York. Some of them are friends of mine. One guy (known as the best street fighter in Flushing) called me outside, saying that I stared at him. That's not true. Anyway, I followed him and his friends to the parking lot where he smashed me a couple of times. I didn't wanna fight him back because he is older than me and I didn't wanna make a big trouble. Two brothers (Kangso and Dongbin) came down and tried to break it up. The problem began because he asked me for respect but he did not give any respect to my old brothers. Then why should I respect him? That's why I jumped in.

The tension has continued between the two groups in New Jersey and in New York. When I asked about the fighting, Joong told me about his feeling and anger about the fighting.

> I am kind of disappointed because they are KP (Korean Power). I thought they are different. They have a good reputation. But, that fighting began with such a small thing. That's nothing. They came back next day. You don't wanna believe this. They called one brother out saying they wanna have a man-to-man talk. But, they beat him up and flew away. I don't understand. They are old, and what are they're fighting for?

The attack on one member is considered as a retaliation for the fighting, which can lead to further tension and ongoing dispute. However, there was no more fighting between the two groups or members. Although some younger brothers, particularly Dojung, wanted to fight back, the older brothers wanted it to be ended. As Joong already mentioned his disappointment in the fighting, older members usually do not fight. The following are general statements on fighting by older members: "It's a kid's thing," "It has been quite a long time since I fought last time," "I do not have to fight anymore," or "We just back up when kids in 9th or 10th grade fight each other." It is usually older members who stop the fighting if it develops to group fighting. Thus, when a member or the group is disrespected, younger members act as a working horse for the group, but limit their actions to inflicting humiliation or beating up an individual, or setting up and engaging in on- on-one fighting for an individual member belonging to a group. Through these episodes, young members spread their victories to nonmembers and maintain a reputation and status. On some occasions, younger members simply engage in the fighting with youth groups in other neighborhoods in order to increase their reputation.

<u>Mugging</u>

After young members joined the group, there emerged a new type of delinquent, who mugged young Korean people. This practice started with the members themselves while they were playing an Internet game in an Internet cafe. When they ran out of money for an Internet game, for instance, they asked one another for one dollar. If other members also ran out of money, they started to ask their friends for one or two dollars. No one asked if they wanted their money back. As time went on, they asked anybody around the Internet café, assuming that young people knew them.

> Outside of an Internet café, Sungjin was sitting on the stairway with Dojung, which blocked the way to the Internet Café, so people had to ask them to give way. Some of the young members were standing outside while talking and playing with one another. Young school-aged boys kept coming in and out of the Internet café. And each time they had to ask if they could cross over where Sungjin and Dojung were sitting. Dojung asked almost every one who went through if he could borrow one dollar. None of them who were asked refused his asking. About thirty or forty minutes after, he counted the

money, and gave two dollars to Sungjin, then went to inside the Internet café. Now it was Sungjin's turn. He repeated exactly the same thing that Dojung did to young people coming to the Internet café. After a while, he also went inside.

While observing, I noticed the pattern of their search for victims. They did not target non-Koreans. If the victims are Korean, they must be young males. They do not see any problem with this activity. The following dialogue describes the practice,

KS: Why are you taking money from kids?

Sungjin: They are my friends. We are in the same school. I just need to buy another hour if time is running out in the middle of the game. I just ask to borrow one dollar.

KS: O.K. Did you pay it back to them?

Sungjin: They don't care about one dollar. They just give it to me if they have money.

KS: What if they don't have money?

Sungjin: Then I just ask another friend. But, if I know he has money, but lied to me that he doesn't, that makes me steamed.

KS: Why?

Sungjin: 'Cause he lied to me. If they don't like to give, then they just need to say so. That's it.

KS: What do you do to that friend?

Sungjin: Well, nothing. I pretty much let him go.

Later, this practice extended to the street and outside of the billiard club on any typical day. The way they asked for money also became more aggressive and threatening. For example, I had to interrupt them one day. They took a young boy to a street corner and searched his body for money. Sungjin smashed the boy's face once, saying, "Get the fuck out of here and never come back." I warned them they could be arrested on a robbery charge. They laughed. Sungjin asked, "How come borrowing one dollar from a friend can be robbery?" This practice became the young members' routine habit.

Other Delinquent Activities

Drug use, fighting, and mugging are engaged in by the whole group or at least by a subgroup of members. Other delinquent behaviors such as gambling, running away, and sexual intercourse are somehow influenced by the group but engaged in by individual members. Dongbin is, as his activities were described in the billiard club, a heavy gambler. Although Kangso, like Dongbin, sometimes plays gambling pool with adults, he is more likely to play a regular pool game with young members. Dongbin's gambling habit leads him to associate with adults in poker games in other billiard clubs where a small room is reserved for gamblers. The adults are usually local retail business owners who often visit billiard clubs to play either pool gambling or poker game. When I asked Dongbin about how the poker game begins and is played, he described, "If at least two people want a poker game, the game can begin. But, four to six people usually play. If less than four, there is always a guy who makes phone calls to people to see if they want to play. So it always begins with at least four people. Before it begins, we set up the money for the day. If it is two thousand dollars for the day, then all have to show their two thousand dollars cash and put it on the table. Minimum is twenty dollars. Whoever loses all his money, he is out. But, if he wants to play again, people always let him in again." He also makes trips to Atlantic City about once a month. He lost a lot of money at the beginning when he learned about gambling. He believes he has made good money four times out of seven.

One of the main topics among members is girls. The way they talk sometimes would be obscene, vulgar, and indecent, although young members are unwilling to reveal their personal sexual preference. Nonetheless, sexual intercourse was more prevalent than members recognized. All members had an experience of sexual relationships with the opposite sex, although there was a great variation in the first time of sexual engagement, ranging from thirteen years of age to seventeen years. Some members had multiple sex partners during a certain period. However, no one used a paid prostitute or went to a room salon or engaged in group sex parties.

Some members had runaway experiences, too. However, since they happened before they joined the group, it should be considered as an individual level of delinquency. The main reason for runaways was conflict with parents. Nonetheless, no one reports that they were forced out of their home by their parents. For instance, Kunsun felt powerless to do much about his relationship with his mom at the time of his runaway. However, he finally found a reasonably comfortable niche in the home when he came back from his second runaway.

CHAPTER 7

The Gang: Mo Ming Pai

The preceding chapter examined the process, structure, and activities of a particular delinquent group in Palisades Park, New Jersey. The gang in Flushing is similar in many respects but also shows considerable differentiation in every key variable the study was searching for. Since a clear distinction between delinquent groups and gangs has not been defined in academic literature, the study differentiated them based on whether a group had a name or not. The operational definition assumes that the name of the group represents the group's effort to mark itself as distinctive and differentiates it from other groups. It is therefore assumed that any group with a name tends to be more organized in its structure and more coherent among its members and is thus engaged more frequently in illegal activities than those without names. The in-depth case analysis will be in the same order that was followed in the last chapter of the delinquent group.

THE GANG STRUCTURE

The gang, Mo Ming Pai, was selected to explore similarities with and differences from a delinquent group in Palisades Park (Please see appendix F for the six members' profiles). The Mo Ming Pai was also chosen because it is one of the Chinese gangs with Korean youth members, who are classified as Twinkies. The Mo Ming Pai in

Mandarin means "no name gang;" the name also implies an interesting phenomenon among emerging gangs that try to hide gang identifications. As seen in the delinquent group analysis, the gang structure cannot be separated from the process of the gang because its size, age of members, membership and leadership are constantly in flux as the gang evolves in its own process.

Size

Unlike the delinquent group, which has a short group life, the accurate size of the Mo Ming Pai gang is somewhat difficult to estimate because of its longevity, which brings it many associates, and also because of the dissociation of some active members from the gang. Since the actual count of the number of members was unknown, the size of the gang was measured based on the active gang members at the time of the data collection period. During the data collection period, about twenty-six active members were in the Mo Ming Pai gang, which was divided into four "generations." Big brothers made up the first and second generations, who were Chinese, except for one Korean member in the second generation. Four out of seven members in the third generation were Koreans. The fourth generation was formed by all three Korean members.

A total of six Korean members participated in the intensive interview process. One Korean member in the second generation, four Korean members in the third generation, and one Korean member in the fourth generation were interviewed. Korean members have been in this gang an average of just under two years. The range varies, including three members who had joined within six months of our conversations, and a member who had been involved for four years. The range of their gang involvement would be much greater if one considered members who had been involved in another gang for a couple of years before they joined the Mo Ming Pai. Although the gang is relatively new compared to major Chinese gangs active in Flushing, it is well known to the residents, law enforcement officers, and young people in the community.

Three characteristics should be noticed here. The first is that the younger the generation is, the more Korean members there are. It remains to be seen whether there will be more Korean members joining the gang in the future. Nonetheless, the pattern of Korean gang members will continue as long as young Koreans are exposed to the

Chinese gang subculture and Korean members in the Mo Ming Pai play a role as recruiters. The second characteristic is that each generation within the gang keep its size as small as possible to maintain positive interdependence. As one member says,

> They (older generation) have friends like I have, you know. We hang out together and do things together, you know. I know some believe they are Mo Ming Pai. But they are not Mo Ming Pai. They are not a part of us. They have to be approved by the members. We don't wanna see anybody in the group. They are just good enough as friends.

There is a clear distinction between associates and members. This limitation of gang membership also seems to enhance cohesiveness among gang members within and between generations. The third characteristic is related to the second characteristic. During the beginning stage of creating a new generation, new members are closely supervised and associated with the last generation until they have seven or eight members to create their own generation. For example, three Chinese with one Korean in the third generation had their membership begun under the second generation until they formed their own generation with three more Korean members. Three Korean members who were newly recruited during the study are now associated with the third generation in their daily activities. However, they are expected to form the fourth generation as they have more new members.

Age

Each generation of the Mo Ming Pai gang is divided by age structure and has a three- or four-year age difference between generations. Although Korean members who participated in the study were not able to confirm their Chinese big brothers' actual ages, they estimated the first generation members are in their late twenties and the second generation are in their mid-twenties. Most members of the third generation are either nineteen or twenty years old, except a Chinese member who is twenty-one years old. In the fourth generation, all three members are seventeen years old. Recall that the delinquent group was principally comprised of adolescents, except two members whose ages were twenty years old in June 2000. In contrast, the Mo Ming Pai gang has more than half of its members over twenty. Another interesting aspect between generational members is that a group of older generation members is living in the same apartment while the younger generation members are living in their individual homes with their families of origin.

Unlike the delinquent group as a typical Fobbie group, where that one-year age difference creates the same-age cliques in the delinquent group and makes a significant impact on membership and relationships among members, there is a much greater age variation within each generation of the Mo Ming Pai, in which members about two or three years apart in age are observed. This age variation in the generations suggests that the age itself does not severely influence relationships among members in the gang. Therefore, older members in the same generation are not considered as Hyung but as friends. The generation, however, does affect the hierarchical relationship between generation members, although it is much looser than in the delinquent group or any other Fobbie group. As a member who had previous experience of a Korea- only gang says,

> When you hang out with Koreans, like if you are Hyung, then you'll pay for everything and take care of young members, like when you go out to places. But if you hang out with Chinese Hyung, they don't necessarily feel like they have to pay for you. So when we hang out as a big group, a lot of times actually, it mostly comes from Hyung, but when we do have to pay, they don't feel like it's a disgrace to ask you for a couple of bucks, like you know. They respect us; it's not that harsh. It's not like Korean tradition. It's very different. Personally, I don't like it (Korean tradition).

Another member also describes the limitation between generations as a way to respect old members:

> We (younger generation members) were never obligated to do things most of the time. But, out of respect, I do certain things for them (older generation members) because I want to. For example, like they have a problem with someone, you know, they ask me to take care of that person with my friends. Like beat them up. But, it's my freedom of choice. I was never obligated to do anything that I did not want to do.

The accounts also imply a difference in terms of behavioral pattern between old and young generations from the delinquent group. As will be seen later, members of an older generation are more likely to be involved in economic crimes such as escort service and credit card fraud, while younger generation members are frequently engaged in violent activities. It is younger members in the third or the fourth generation who go on missions, which usually involve settling a score with rival gang members in rumble-fistfights, but often pipes and clubs are added to the mix. Younger generation members also are heavily engaged in street drug selling and mugging.

Membership through Peer Network

Korean Mo Ming Pai members obtained their membership through school or a neighborhood peer network as was observed in the delinquent group. However, they differ because Korean members in the Chinese Mo Ming Pai must be initiated through Chinese friends. Although a Korean member in the second generation does not recruit other Koreans, more Korean members are recruited by Korean members in the third and the fourth generations. I will elaborate in detail how Koreans get into the Chinese gang later, but a simple description will help to understand membership through peer network. For example, Don recruited two Korean members, Hana and Sam, whom he knew through a private education institute. While the members hung out in a billiard club, they recruited Matt, who was a former Korean Power gang member. As the chain of referral expanded, Matt brought two more members, whom he knew from when he had Korean Power gang membership.

This network process illustrates that although the first two Korean members in the second generation of the Mo Ming Pai had to have a connection with a Chinese member to get into the gang, the majority of Korean members obtained their memberships through Korean members with whom they already had established social ties, such as education or previous gang experience. This preexisting social tie also implies that the boundary of the network is wider compared to the delinquent group. For example, all members in the delinquent group were from one of two neighborhood school zones, while Korean members in Mo Ming Pai are comprised of Korean youths from outside the Flushing neighborhood. Another interesting feature is that, compared to the delinquent group in which six members are linked through kinship, no

Korean members in the Mo Ming Pai gang informed me that there was any kinship with one another.

Gender

No female gang members are found in the Mo Ming Pai. A description that is more accurate would be that they are not allowed to join the gang. It becomes clear with a member's illustration of the gang's brotherhood:

> I could personally tell you this much about MMP. We weren't much about girls. Different gangs have different images. We're mostly about brotherhood, hanging out and having fun, you know. Even before I joined the MMP, I knew it was more about brotherhood. That's what I like about it.

Nonetheless, girls are involved in escort services or credit card fraud. A member says that younger generation members are engaged in delivering escort service girls to sites where clients stay. The other members also say that they use their girlfriends to pick up items delivered by credit card fraud to buy items using fraudulent checks with fake I.D.s. In comparison, it should be noted that the escort service girls are different from the girls labeled "gulrae" who associate with the delinquent group in Palisade Park. While the delinquent group members exploit the girls with the label "gulrea" as sex objects for themselves, the Mo Ming Pai gang members use girls or girlfriends for credit card fraud and escort services as partners in the gang business. More details will be provided in the section on the gang activities.

Leadership

Each generation has its own leaders while older generation leaders often extend their leadership over the younger generation members. Unlike the delinquent group where younger members recognize all older members as "Hyung," or leaders, any member who is actively engaged in the gang activity is considered a leader, regardless of the age difference. As a member of the third generation states, "If you're not active, you're not recognized as a leader of the generation." When he was asked about the leader of his generation, he says, "Sonny would be the one, because he brought members when our generation first started and he is most active in the group." Based on accounts by three participants, due to his heavy involvement in the older generation's gang business, Sonny often connects younger members to the older generation's business. Members of the older generations usually do not have enough time or opportunity to build cohesiveness with members of the younger generations during their routine activity, although they frequently encounter younger members in regular hangout places. Therefore, to a certain extent Sonny's leadership is critical in bringing different generation members together. In fact, the three Korean members in the third generation were asked by Sonny on behalf of the older generation if they were interested in working in gambling, credit card fraud, check fraud, or the escort services.

In general, the younger generations are often considered as a work force, which will be described in the section on gang activities and the younger generation's role of manpower, from the older generation's perspective. As a second generation member says:

> Many (older generation members) are usually behind any violent scene. See, if one of us, say, got a beef (trouble) with someone or a group of people, simply (young generation members are) more likely to end up beating up that person or group fighting.

THE YOUTH GANG PROCESS

As in the delinquent group process, the analysis of the youth gang process is divided into three different stages: getting into the Chinese gang, persistence, and desistance. The stage of getting into the Chinese gang examines the conditions for the emergence and development of Korean cliques within the gang. The persistence stage focuses on how the gang controls its Korean members and continues its existence for the furtherance of its interests. Finally, the desistance stage discusses reasons for some Korean members to leave the gang.

Getting into the Chinese gang

In the description of general characteristics of the gangs, I explained that Korean youth living in the Flushing Korean community must have had a great exposure to Asian gangs, compared to those in the Palisades Park Korean community. To measure personal exposure to gangs in the community and its impact, each member was asked his personal feeling toward and his experience with various gangs before he joined the gang. Through their oral histories, six Mo Ming Pai Korean members provided three general themes of exposure to gangs: daily observation of the presence of gangs in the community, the popularity of gangs among Korean teenagers, and interpersonal conflicts with gang members. In varying degrees, all six members mentioned their daily observation of gangs and gang members since they were young. At the extreme, Hana explains,

> I saw them (Korean and Chinese gang members) in school everyday. After school when walking down to Northern Boulevard, I saw gang members again hanging out in front of pool halls and cafes. I even knew one brother in the church my parents and I used to attend was a gang member and saw him in Sunday school in the church.

Sam, the best friend of Hana, provides the other aspect of gang exposure in the neighborhood. His statement also summarizes very well how a negative attitude about gangs can be changed to a positive one among young Koreans who are exposed to gangs in the community:

> When you live in this neighborhood, you hear many things about gangs. People say bad things about them and if you were a kid, you believed these things until your good friends became gang members. They (friends) would tell you about friendship, parties and places to go, and a feeling of pride in the gang. Some of them always talked about gang fighting and stories too. They said they jumped into the fighting because they are brothers, which I say what the hell was wrong with that? After all, they are not that bad at all.

These statements demonstrate that it is inevitable for young Koreans to observe a certain amount of gang activities and talk about gang stories in the neighborhood. Although Sam does not elaborate, a part of his statement--"always talked about gang fighting and stories"--

indicates the popularity of gangs among Korean teens in the community as well. As another member, Willie, clearly states,

> Gangs are very attractive. You see all the smart kids ending up joining gangs. Some of them were really popular among us. When they actually join the gang, the gang now becomes more popular. Almost everyone joined because they knew someone in it. You see what I mean, gangs are a popular thing instead of a survival thing to us.

He continues, "I am pretty sure you would say we are not a gang, because most gangs come from bad families. We are regular kids, we have money, we don't need to rob people." His statement conveys the idea that the gang -at least the one he belongs to- is different from the image of inner city gangs that often have gang members from poor ethnic minorities. It should also be noted that Korean gang members often claim that smart or regular kids join their gang. There is a tendency for gang members to use this as an excuse, saying how popular the gang is among Korean high school students and expressing a good aspect of gangs at the same time.

In such a neighborhood where a high level of gang exposure exists, interpersonal conflict such as one-on-one fighting often leads individual Koreans to join the gang and engage in gang fighting. Another member, Don, provides a good example. He describes three fights he got into with Vietnamese students in school before he joined the gang. The fighting began because of a group of Korean students being called "gooks," a derogatory epithet toward Koreans, by a Vietnamese student. At the first fight, there was no evidence of his direct motivation to join the gang. However, the fact that the Vietnamese student showed up with gang members made him seek help from other gang members. As he explains,

> About a year ago, I heard the Vietnamese guy I knew, say these fucking gooks don't know any better. I answered that he ought to know better than to say something like that and that he was a real fake chink, pretending to be a Chinese. One thing led to another, and we finally had a fight. The next day, he brought his FD (Flying Dragon) friends. It was stupid to fight myself against a bunch of these guys, so I tried to run

away. But, they got me after school. I don't want to talk
about what really happened. It was the worst day in my life.
They even said they would kill me if they see me again. Then,
I asked Sonny (a Chinese friend and Mo Ming Pai gang
member) to help. Back then, he and I were not that close but
we became good friends after that.

The friendship Don developed with the Chinese Mo Ming Pai gang
member played an important role in his association with the Mo Ming
Pai gang. His case provides a part of answer to the question of how he
eventually got into the gang. Recall that the fight between Dojung and
four Korean boys in the delinquent group of Palisades Park, led them to
join the group. Interpersonal violence among young Koreans is seen as
a common factor for both members in the delinquent group and the
gang to decide to join or to be accepted in the group. However, if
young Koreans in Flushing were assumed to have similar risk factors to
be gang members, why did so many Korean youths choose Chinese
gangs instead of Korean gangs? The members were also asked how
they initially got into the gang.

James was the first Korean member in the Mo Ming Pai. He
stopped schooling at age fourteen and started to hang out with other
dropouts. As he says, "There was nothing to do much. I was just
hanging out and making friends with guys like me, who always got in
trouble at school. Then I started getting into drugs and stealing and
parties." He associated with different gangs as a peripheral member
until he found more comfort with the Mo Ming Pai members. He
continues, "Back then, people say I'm GS, I'm FD, Bulla, Bulla, Bulla.
Like them, I was looking for something and I felt pretty good as I hung
around with them (Mo Ming Pai members) more and more."

Willie was the second Korean Mo Ming Pai member, but he was
the one of the first four members who started the third generation. Like
Don, he was introduced into the gang through the same Chinese gang
member, Sonny. His illustration also provided how the third generation
within the Mo Ming Pai was started. He and Sonny were good school
friends before Sonny joined the Mo Ming Pai. He recalls,

I had some close Chinese friends in school. Sonny was my
best friend since ninth grade. When I became a tenth grade,
my friends were mostly all Chinese. Not that I pick them that
way, but they just happened to be around. There were four of

us hanging out together (he was the only Korean)...Sonny brought us to one of the big brothers' apartment. I guess we had a good time, you know. I just liked so much of the stuff we did with them. And big brothers treated us right, you know. I felt like I was a part of them. Then, all of us happened to pledge our brotherhood.

Although Willie and Don attended the same school, all they knew about each other was the Korean ethnicity they had in common. As was described, it was through Sonny, who had many Chinese and Korean friends in the school that the two Korean members initially got into the gang at different times. However, they became best friends after becoming members. By the time Don joined the gang, the Mo Ming Pai needed more members due to the escalation of a conflict with other Chinese gangs. As a result, the gang aggressively recruited two more Korean members, which led the third generation to have its own grouping independent from the big brothers in the second generation. It means that although the third generation is under the influence of the older generation, it has its own age-graded structure and activities.

Don played a key role in recruiting two more Korean youths, whom he met first in a private education institute. Although Don stopped going to the institute, he remembered that Hana and Sam had cocky attitudes, which led him to believe that they might be interested in joining the gang. However, both Hana and Sam revealed that they had experienced a period of confusion, doubt, and struggle regarding their membership when Don asked them to join the gang. For instance, although Hana had many friends in the Korean Power gang, he didn't join the gang because he thought gangs were dangerous and risky at that time. As he says,

I saw many in trouble in the KP. I was not quite sure what they (Mo Ming Pai) were up to. So, I just hung out with them. Then, one day, they were going to have a meeting and asked us to join. Sam and I did not know what to do at that time. Then, Don said something like, 'Come on, what are you guys waiting for? Let's go.' That was a lot of help us to make a decision right away. At the meeting, there was an issue of a girl and FD. And, they told us things to do and things not to do. And I guess we were MMP after the meeting.

However, since the Mo Ming Pai gang had no initiation to accept members, the question of how long they stayed in the gang varied according to individual members who believed they were accepted or decided to join the gang. Sam provided a different story of the time when he believed he had joined the gang. He said, "I was interested in it and hung out with them. But I wasn't really in it because I didn't act like a Mo Ming Pai member....or acknowledge it....I was scared because it was too much for me at that time." He added, "But things happened rather quickly. One day MMP members saw a member of the FD at a pool hall. I was just there. They dragged him outside and beat him. A week later, I was hanging out at Pro Billiards when seven members of the FD walked in. They caught me alone and they got me. I couldn't help it, and I was in." After that incident, he gained respect in members' eyes by having being heavily outnumbered and badly beaten.

I interviewed one member of the fourth generation, which began in the mid-1998. Three members of the fourth generation were Koreans and were recruited at the same time. This time Hana as a facilitator contacted Matt, who used to live in the S.H. apartment building and was an ex-Korean Power gang member. To Matt, the Mo Ming Pai was a new avenue to spend his time and energy on a daily basis. He explained,

> After a couple of KP big brothers were arrested, we saw ourselves break up. Members still hung out, but big brothers (in the Korean Power gang) asked me to stay away from them. This was not the reason that I joined Mo Ming Pai. I was sick of the "Sunbae thing" you know. There was a lot of respect thing going on between Sunbae and Hoobae by the time I started hanging out with Hana and his friends. They are older than me, but we are just like friends, you know.

He also brought two more Korean Power gang members into the Mo Ming Pai with him. When members were asked about their perception of Chinese members, responses was very positive, and they felt a strong bond regardless of the difference in ethnicity. Following are good examples of their statements.

We are really friends. Sometimes, we would call the Chinese guys chinks and they would call us gooks, but it was just fun.

I get along with them. I like them because there are no Korean ideas at all there. They have a respect thing like KP. But it's loose. As long as you do not cross the line, you can really enjoy it in the group. The idea is that we are all one, like real brothers.

I often felt more comfortable hanging out with them than with my Korean friends. That doesn't mean they are better than my Korean friends. Well....I never have bothered whether anybody was Korean or Chinese. No matter who I was with, I have never discussed this kind of stuff because it doesn't matter. If I liked the fellow, I made friends with him, no matter what race he was.

While becoming gang members, the Korean youths in the Mo Ming Pai have many common paths shared with the delinquent group in Palisades Park, New Jersey. For example, the third generation of the Mo Ming Pai gang started with school friends. Then, it expanded its members through networks outside school settings such as private education institutes and community entertainment facilities. What is probably significant, compared to the delinquent groups, the majority of Korean gang members acknowledge rather indifferently the fact of their gang memberships in the Chinese gang. In other words, although most of the Korean gang members have known or been involved in Korean ethnic gangs, they are quite willing to join Chinese gangs that have a better reputation among Korean youths, that accepted them on an equal basis, and that did not demand any great change in their cultural habits. The fact that they do not venture outside the neighborhood for friends can simply be attributed to the ethnic composition of the neighborhood in which they live. In Flushing, as described, Chinese and Koreans are two dominating groups who share many socio-cultural characteristics and interact easily through daily routine activities. For this reason, even though Korean gang members to a certain extent adopted many American lifestyles and youth cultures, they choose to become involved in Chinese gangs rather than other ethnic gangs.

Interestingly, except for the first three Chinese members in the third generation, no more Chinese gang members were actively recruited. Although the fourth generation is developing and only one Korean member was interviewed, all three members in the fourth generation are Koreans. There is no doubt that culturally determined similarities in behavior and ethnicity probably are of importance among some Korean gang members who initially affiliated with Chinese gangs. However, these hardly provide a complete explanation for the development of a clique consisting of Koreans in a Chinese gang. It should be noticed that Korean gang members have had some Chinese friends, but their friends have been predominantly of Korean ethnicity. During the same time, interview data indicated an abundance of Korean youths at risk, and the existence of peer networks among Korean youths outside school settings in the community where Korean youths are easily recruited into Chinese gangs through Korean gang members. In sum, compared to the delinquent group in Palisades Park, Korean members in the Mo Ming Pai had observed activities of both Chinese and Korean gangs in their neighborhood. This daily observation intensified the popularity of these gangs among Korean youths. In the context of a neighborhood like Flushing, Twinkie Korean youths who often express indifference about Chinese and Korean ethnicity tend to join Chinese gangs.

Persistence

If the delinquent group persists mainly through delinquent entertainment activities, the Mo Ming Pai persists through its new emerging generations. The term 'generation' is used among the members for age-graded groupings within the gang. As Matt describes,

> There is the first generation, second, third and now the fourth. The second generation follows the first generation. The third follows the second. The fourth follows the third and on it goes. Generations they go by, like first members are like first generation. And then, members that joined after them, after that group of people, they are just second, third and the fourth generation.

Although the Mo Ming Pai unites as a group through entertainment as does the delinquent group, the gang also keeps evolving through illegal money-generating activities developed by older generation members. When considering gang business, the younger generation members are used as a work force according to the older generation's viewpoint. As James explains the relationship between old and young generations:

> There is a usage because you always rely on' em (young generation members) for manpower. If we have conflict and we need to fight somebody or shake down somebody, we might call them as muscle but otherwise they are not involved with older generation business. You see, they might help but they won't come out and do actual activity. For example, if I am doing extortion, I go and talk to the owner. I won't need them to go and talk to the owner but just be outside. If you are involved in something like robbery, you might not need them. If you need them, you just call upon them. Sometimes you know they're needed as bases. Ones who are actually involved in the old generation. They are the ones who are making the money and earning the money because they have expenses. Younger generation, they go home and bring the money out and spend. So we are not actually supporting them in a financial sense ...so there is a necessity to have a younger generation to maintain muscle power or strength of the group. But the strength of the group comes from the financial backbone.

This generational difference is also found in the type of living accommodation. As described earlier, a group of the older generation members is living together in the same apartment while they allow younger generation members to stay at their individual homes. James explains the reason,

> Just say going out and trying and paying money, it's almost impossible for us to financially maintain all our younger members. So it's preferable if we have many living at home so we are not financially burdened by them. In the younger generation, a lot face family problems or they just don't wanna

stay at home. Their father might beat them or they always be criticized about their thing or their parents are divorced or their parents are fighting. They wanna avoid that situation. We allow these individuals to come out of home and provide housing for them and expenses. But a lot of kids, they have a steady home. They do good at school. They just wanna associate with the group. They are more preferable for us. You see if they leave home, sometimes they create more problems, such as a parent might come out looking for them or they might go to the police. It would be too much burden. So we leave them at home but we use these individuals in need as bases.

James continues,

Talk about young generations, they wanna join the gang. They associate with the group as a fun source or a group identity. They feel like they belong to the group or they belong to some kind of association. That's attractive for them. In that sense, they come into the group but they're not participating fully with the older generation's business.

This generational difference becomes clear with younger generation members' responses when asked about older generation business. For example, Hana said, "I personally don't know cause I never asked them like what they do or never went to them for help on how can I make money. I personally don't know much about it. But, I am sure there is a large quantity of drugs and extortion. They have connections with a few bars and clubs; they provide protection or manage them and share the money." Another young generation member, Willie, adds, "They (old generation) have no reason talking about their business in front of us. I usually see them over the weekend and the time we're drinking or clubbing. We talk about what's going on outside, like who would get into fighting, like very small talk."

These statements can be interpreted as the older generation maintaining its members for financial reasons, while younger generation continues through a sense of belonging and fun. Recall a younger generation member's description: "We're mostly about brotherhood, hanging out and having fun, you know." The following are responses of other younger generation members about their daily group activities: "Just randomly hanging out in Flushing like in parks and pool halls and through friends," we "basically do nothing. Hang out in pool halls, drinking alcohol or hangout in friend's house, use drugs," or "I do the things they do. We have the same interests, like not going to school, using drugs, and beat up people, drinking and hang out all the time. That's why I hang out with'em." To the younger generation, therefore, non-financial activities, such as having fun and hanging out, are necessary to support the gang's continuance, as was observed earlier in the delinquent group.

It is important to notice that the older generation also started with non-financial reasons such as unity. As James explains,

> I can't tell you how the first generation started. But I tell you the second generation started, in a sense, with bonding, you know. You feel like you belong to a group. You have a friend because friendship is emphasized and brotherhood and loyalty are emphasized. When these are emphasized, you feel like a part of something.... You have a bond with eight to ten gang members. You are very close, best friends, best friends, best friends. You are highly unified among members. Ah... I don't know how to describe this. It's just about hang out then. It's also a sense of avoidance of responsibility....so in a sense, neglecting school responsibility, and some kind of having fun and a way of socializing.

This bond as a reason to join and form the gang habituates members to a gang life-style, which creates family problems and causes members to leave their homes. James explains the circumstances in which older generation members leave their homes and live as a group in an apartment:

> Many (the first and second generation) are able to and they are old enough so they just leave home because it's more convenient for them. If you are coming out of home to go to a party at 12 or 1 o'clock in the morning and coming back home that night, you'll be in a lot of conflict at home so it's preferable if you live outside. Otherwise, you'll always be questioned, like your mom would say, where have you been and who have you been with, so it creates a lot of conflicts.

This creates a situation where older generation members seek out financial resources to maintain continuity, as they get older and independent financially. James continues about why older generation members need to secure themselves financially:

> They live outside home. They live by themselves or by groups in an apartment. To do this, you need a stable income because you can't afford rent or bills. To bring in income, you operate any criminal activity. Like I said, our gang starts with a group of people, around five to ten people, who are most actively involved. Just actively recruiting younger generation members makes the group become very large. Here, it's not necessary that all the members be actively engaged in criminal activity.

James clearly points out that the gang persists through the attraction of money- generating criminal activities, despite some evidence of other reasons to affiliate younger generation members with the gang in terms of non-money generating gang activities. It seems that different driving forces exist to maintain the different generations within the gang. Again, the younger generation has similar activities that continue their association with one another, just like the delinquent group. Nonetheless, as the gang lasts longer and members remain longer in the gang, the financial resources are necessary to keep the gang intact.

Desistance

Unlike the delinquent group where the group was analyzed from its emergence to the breakdown of the group as a whole, the gang continues as long as the next generation evolves and follows the generation before. Thus, the desistance is examined here as individual Korean members dissociate from the gang. The best way to describe why a particular gang member leaves the gang at a particular time is to compare it to the delinquent group members. Whereas the delinquent group members experience a natural breakdown of the group for positive reasons, the gang members are forced to cease their participation in the gang due to negative reasons. For instance, joining the army, having a job and preparing for college were main reasons for the delinquent members to leave, while incarceration or arrest experiences are the first reason for the gang members' dissociation from the gang. For example, a member with three of his friends, who can be defined as peripheral members, was arrested for aiding in the homicide of a Korean taxi driver while they planned a robbery. The person who actually committed the homicide was held at Rikers Island while the case was still in court during the data collection period. Details will be provided of the gang activity. The following responses obtained from two members who were dissociating from the gang are representative of the reasons why they left, although some additional reasons are included.

> One time I got arrested for fighting. They (police) had pictures and knew who's who. Then I see my parents working very hard for me and want what's best for me and having always a little Christian life on the side that I never paid attention to, like you know. I realize and see God.

> I was working in gambling house. One of the clients borrowed $10,000. I was told to have that loan paid. I and several friends went and took him out of his house and held him and ask him to pay the debt. I was arrested for that but released because I was not involved in major criminal activity. But my parents had to pay a high lawyer's fee, and I had kind of matured, too.

Interestingly, two members above mentioned maturing and religious conversion as reasons to break away from the gang. Chapter 8 will discuss religious conversion in detail as a part of policy implication. The members also mentioned that getting out of the gang is individual free choice and no punishment is imposed. Therefore, it is relatively easy if members are willing to disaffiliate. Nonetheless, members experience, in reality, difficulty in breaking the bond with the gang completely because of the maintenance of personal contact with current gang members. As Willie illustrates, "I don't wanna do things I used to do anymore. Sometimes, I hang out with them but I am not active with them. I just keep in touch with a couple of people I personally like.... I don't regret what I did because that's who I am and where I am now."

THE YOUTH GANG ACTIVITIES

Compared to the delinquent group, gang members report greater involvement in criminal activities. The gang members commit delinquent acts such as substance abuse, fighting and mugging, just as the delinquent group does. However, the two groups differ because the gang members also participate in serious offenses such as drug sales, robbery, escort services, weapon possession, and credit card fraud. Among the serious offenses that the gang members commit, drugs are sold by individual members while other serious offenses are usually committed by a group of gang members, consisting of two to five members, rather than by the whole group. Moreover, there is clear distinction between the older generation and younger generation regarding gang activities they are engaged in. As you will see, the fighting, mugging, and a small amount of street drug selling are the younger generation members' main activities, though some older generation members are also involved in escort service, credit card, and check fraud activities.

Drugs

Drug Selling

The main difference in drug activity compared to the delinquent group is that individual gang members sell drugs. Three out of six members interviewed reported they never sold illegal drugs. According to them, older generation members deal a large amount of drugs whereas younger generation members sell comparatively a small amount of drugs. James, the second-generation member differentiates his previous involvement in selling a large amount of drugs with the younger generation's individual drug-selling.

> You see drugs coming in and controlled by primarily Chinese members, and the younger generation does not see action. You can't sell the drugs unless you have a drug connection. I know a lot of younger generation selling drugs, but not kilos, a large quantity, because the connection isn't there. They can't deal in kilos of heroin or just say marijuana and distribute them. In a large sense, what they are able to do is to deal a

small amount of drugs on the street. I don't believe all of them (younger generation) are involved. Only a couple of members actually sell drugs.

However, it is to be noted that the drug business has become less lucrative to older generation members today. According to James, it is due to cheaper drugs brought in by different nationals such as Mexicans and to the heavy crackdown by law enforcement. This change in the Asian drug market results in shifting their attention to other illegal business such as escort services and credit card fraud. This change also pushed some older generation members to establish themselves through legal business in the community. As he points out, "Believe or not, some made a lot of money and now own a small business so they don't want to get their hands dirty."

His observation regarding drug dealing by younger generation members is accurate as an insider. Following is the conversation with Matt, who sells drugs on a regular basis.

KS: How much do you make out of a drug sale?

Matt: There were very few occasions I made like a thousand dollars at one deal. But I usually collect about four hundred or five hundred dollars a week.

KS: Can you tell me the types of drugs you sell?

Matt: Usually marijuana and some Ecstasy But, it was mostly marijuana for me.

KS: Have you ever been arrested for drug selling?

Matt: No, I never got arrested for selling drugs although I almost got arrested a couple of times.

KS: To whom did you sell them?

Matt: Mostly friends. Actually half of the time it's my friends. The other half are people that know that I sell drugs who call me.

KS: How do they know you sell them?

Matt: Word spreads, like if my friends go on drugs and they have friends. It's like a chain reaction with their friends and whatever.

KS: Can you tell me about actual drug transactions?

Matt: What do you mean?

KS: I mean, how you hand over drugs to people who want them.

Matt: It's simple. If I'm delivering it, I personally give it to them and receive the money from them hand-to-hand or I drop it off and they just pick it up from wherever I am.

KS: Is there any particular spot where you like to sell them?

Matt: There is no place I do it. It's wherever I'm located at that time and that was usually pool halls, because that's where I hang out all the time. I know Don (another member) does it in the PC bank. He's there, like I am in pool halls. I'm not very...I don't like games. I'm not very much a game person so I don't hang out there much. Otherwise, it usually where you are or like you are halfway, me be there and meet you, like random places, you know.

Although younger generation members deal with a small amount of drugs, they view their drug selling activity as a viable means of making money, like the older generation members. This interpretation is supported by a statement made by another member, Willie who engaged in drug selling to have money for gang recreational activities. He explains, "You got to have money for going out and kicking and whatever. And you're not gonna ask money from your parents every single day so you end up either mugging or selling drugs." Although their profits out of drug sales were often shared through recreational activities, members again reported that their drug sales are for individual profit. There is clearly a different point of view between older generation and younger generation regarding drug selling.

<u>Drug Abuse</u>

Like the delinquent group members, the gang members use drugs as well. The heavy alcohol consumption is also similar in both groups. Although both groups abuse illicit drugs, the gang is much active in terms of the frequency of drug abuse, compared to the delinquent group. For example, the most popular drug is marijuana. All six gang members reported that they smoke marijuana almost every day. Two indicate they smoke at least three times a day. The second most popular drug is Ecstasy, which five members used over the weekend in Manhattan nightclubs. Two reported that they also use other drugs in addition to marijuana and Ecstasy. Their favorite type of drug differs, based on their experience with drugs. As one member says, "For me, mushroom is my favorite because it is the mildest form of acid so I am able to control my high. I enjoy it very much because I feel like I am in different world. It is not reality. I feel like I am shipped to another planet. It is different." Another member whose favorite is special K explains how to use it: "It's powerful. I mean it's stronger than the others. It's in a liquid form, so you either blow-dry it or microwave it or you could fry it, and then you turn it into powder form, and then you sniff it."

The following conversation illustrates the types of drugs used and their source:

KS: Have you ever used any drugs?

Don: I have used marijuana, Ecstasy, mushroom, coke, and special K.

KS: How do you get them?

Don: My friends or like some dealers I know.

KS: Do "friends" mean Mo Ming Pai members?

Don: Not always, like random people I know who sell. Bronx

or uptown, and you go over there. You go to the street and
there they sell. They're selling drugs, like you know. You go
up to them, you know. You ask them, you know. You have
this or do you have that. Then they give it to you. It's easy
but I'm not doing this because it's dangerous. Cause a couple
of my friends got arrested after giving them drugs because
those are known spots, you know.... What else do we do with
a bunch of black people? So they know we were there to get
drugs, you know. When they see us, they keep an eye on us
there, you know. It's easy to get arrested because it's a hot
spot. That's why I don't like going over there.

KS: How much do people pay for it?

Don: It depends on the amount. $20 for a bag of marijuana.

Violence

Fighting

A comparison of the delinquent group and the gang's fighting further
differentiates the two groups. Whereas one-on-one fighting is popular
among the delinquent group members, group fighting, in which two or
more members engage in the fighting, is popular in the gang. While
delinquent group members set up the place and time for the one-on-one
fighting, the gang members who engage in group fighting do so
spontaneously, usually because they are intoxicated.. The following is
a description of the typical group-fighting situation:

> When you're drinking. .... Especially when you go out
> drinking, you're hanging out with bunch of friends. That, you
> know, it's group of people. Other people also have groups of
> friends themselves. And, like people get drunk, like you know,
> some people act like different. They can't control themselves.
> And, they act hard-core and stuff like that. And then, you see
> yourself jumping up, and getting into the fight.

Interestingly, gang members overreact when they are together. As
Sam points out, "There is more sense of self-extinction, I say. If you

are by yourself, you feel like I don't wanna do that, I don't wanna go and talk to him. But, if you're in a group and friends behind you, you feel more brave. You feel I could just go and be tough. If you have other members, because my friends are looking at me, I have to respond." This statement is similar to that of Joong in the delinquent group, saying that he had to stand up against schoolteachers or adults because young members are watching him.

The motivation for fighting is often trifling, such as staring or verbal provocation. However, there is no particular gang or group that the Mo Ming Pai gang has conflicts with. As Hana explains,

> You might look at my girlfriend or we might go to the club, you might bump into me or I might bump to you. You look at me wrong, I might look at you wrong, and conflict arises. You see. If I'm in a bar and you're in a bar, we are sitting and drinking and you sitting and drinking, and I am looking over my shoulder and I'm looking at you and you are looking at me. You see face-to-face, eye-to-eye, and that creates conflict, so I might get up and say, why you looking at me or some kind of words might be exchanged and in that sense, a fighting broke out.

Therefore, it can be anybody and any group of people. What seems to be a mere trifle often leads to a serious incident, which then again sets up ongoing intergang fighting. For example, there was an incident at a local bar where eight Mo Ming Pai members clashed with about thirty Flying Dragon gang members, and a total of six people were hospitalized out of that melee. As Willie says, "After that, we had a beef with FD; we heard they were driving around looking for us. So five of us got in a car with machetes and drove around. Luckily we didn't find them."

The other difference compared to the delinquent group is that the gang members admit gun and other weapons possession. Members were asked the types of weapons they carry and the reasons to carry them. The following conversation illustrates:

KS: Do you use weapons?

Matt: Sometimes we carry guns like a week or so. Mostly machetes or a pocket knife.

KS: Have you ever used them?

Matt: No. I haven't used them.

KS: Why do you carry them?

Matt: For protection, I personally didn't use it because I didn't need to. (He shows his machete.) When I carried it, I didn't have any trouble. But my friends that have carried them, they have used them. When I took it out, it was very intimidating, yeah. That was good enough to show off half of the time. But the other half, you use it when you have to use it.

KS: Are there any other weapons?

Matt: There is also a baton or a pipe; members use it.

Guns are not the preferred weapon because of the frequent stops and searches from the police. Guns are usually carried for a short period, or only one person carries the gun when there is a conflict with another gang. Due to the availability of these weapons and overreaction among members to trivial matters, serious and unplanned fighting often results.

<u>Robbery</u>

There are two types of robbery popular among gang members: home invasion and taxi robbery. Gang members consider these criminal activities as a source of steady income. As James says:

> The group all wanna form some kind of business, either illegal or legal. Unless you have a large amount of money coming in, there is no steady income…. The group can't extort, no drug trading and no illegal immigrant smuggling, so what the group depends on is robbery. So you see, the increase of robbery is because that's the only way to earn the money and robbery is fairly simple. If you have a gun or if you could mug someone, that's the income because there is no other form of rackets or vices.

His statement explains that robbery as a source of income gained its popularity among the gang members after the change of the illegal opportunity structure, in which no other criminal activities were available to the gang in the community. His simple analysis implies that robbery is popular because it is readily available. It also implies that the existence of the gang, which is either characterized by having fun or focusing on money generating, will continue unless we prevent them in early stage of development.

When asked for the method of a robbery, members experienced in home invasion robbery say that they select their target through a tip, and then three or four members form a group to invade the target's home. For example, James says, "You see, somebody might say that person owned a busy restaurant. We think that person may have a lot of money. We follow that person to see where he lives." Because many Koreans use a personal loan, "Kae-Don," they target the individual who makes the personal loan. James continues, "A lot of "Kae-Don" were very popular. If one of the members knew a person who has a lot of Kae-Don, we might try to invade that home. We just take a guess." When asked about the planning of the robbery, he said, "It was very short planning and very simple. We hear a tip. Then, we go around four or five to where they live. The target is not jewelry or a T.V. It's not a burglary. It's robbery."

The other popular method is to rob Korean cab drivers. The reason for taxi robbery is, first, Korean taxi drivers always have relatively large amounts of cash, and, second, they usually do not report the incident to police because many are not registered for taxi service and many have undocumented immigration status. The typical plan is simple. For example, a gang member will call up a taxi service from the Korean Yellow Pages and tell the driver to make a pick-up, a member who usually has the plainest facial features of the group and is the least likely to arouse suspicion at a particular street corner. Then, the member gets into the cab and tells the driver to take him a couple of miles away to a street, usually a dead-end street in a quiet residential area, where no one is around except the other gang members who wait until the taxi arrives. The member in the cab usually holds up the driver with a nine-millimeter handgun while the other members grab the driver's cash and walkie-talkie, so the driver cannot call for help. Then, the gang members get back into their car and drive away. Handguns are usually carried for threatening the cab driver. However, things can happen in an unexpected way. On June 16, 1998, four

Korean youngsters, including three Mo Ming Pai members, planned to rob a cab driver. However, the plan went wrong and ended up with the killing of the driver, Hyung Kyu Kim, a 43-year old Korean immigrant who was working the graveyard shift for the ABC Call Taxi service in Flushing.

According to the Queens District Attorney's statement issued shortly after Frank's arrest, "There was a struggle and the defendant shot Mr. Kim (the cab driver) in the right side of the neck. The bullet entered and went through Mr. Kim's neck, killing him and exiting and grazing the defendant's left arm."

<u>Mugging</u>

While robbery requires weapons, automobiles, and tips, mugging does not require them and it is readily available. Mugging is very popular among younger generation members. However, it is generally discouraged by the older generation members as a reckless thing. James describes the generational difference:

> I could approach another student or child, and push him around. It doesn't even need a gun or knife. You just drag them and beat them up and mug them. That's, in a sense, income. If I mug five people today, I could come up with $100 or $200. With that money, we go easy out and have fun. It's low level of forming income. With the older group, they have other ways of bringing income. That's why they don't go out and mug people. They have escort services or other businesses bringing $1,000 to $5,000 a week to the group. If you have that kind of income, you don't need mugging people. If you're twenty to twenty-one, in that age group, you have other activities that bring more money because it's too risky.

Unlike robbery, which is done by three or four members as a team, mugging is usually done alone. When asked about the frequency, victim, and process of the mugging, Matt says,

> I used to mug every day. I see people on the street. I have a couple of incidents that I mugged adults but mostly they were kids my age or older. I don't need a gun or machete to mug

kids. I go up to them and ask, "Run your shit or give me root," and they usually say no. And, then smack with trick. For example, if there is a group of kids, pick the biggest kid, and kick him or punch him bad enough to make sure that he really gets hurt. That's only way it goes easy. You really take control over other kids, too, you know.

Non-Traditional Crimes

The most conspicuous gang activities are non-traditional crimes such as credit card fraud, check fraud, or escort services. In each crime activity, two to five members participate rather than the whole gang. With this analysis of the non-traditional crimes, the role of older and younger generations should be noted. The younger generation members play the role of chauffeur for transportation of escort service girls to clients or as receiver and/or sender of illicit items obtained through credit card or check frauds, while older generation members manage escort service girls or gather credit card/check numbers and names of the identity theft victims through stolen credit card receipts or stolen checks.

Credit Card Fraud

The gang members are involved in numerous fraudulent purchases of merchandise by stolen credit cards, either in stores or via the Internet. However, the credit card fraud scheme through the Internet is more popular and has been done as follows. The gang members purchase various laptop or other high-end electronic items via computer or electronic company's websites or Internet auction companies. The items, which are purchased utilizing stolen credit card accounts, are shipped overnight via express courier companies. Gang members use various shipping addresses, such as those of their friends or any Queens or Bronx neighbors who are normally not in their home during daytime. They put the tracking number for the item in the courier's website to see the time the item is delivered. Then, younger generation members park in their automobile in front of the shipping address, waiting for delivery of the item. When a parcel carrier puts the item outside the door, the younger generation members simply pick it up. Otherwise, the member or his girlfriend shows up before a parcel carrier leaves with the item and signs for the package and accepts it.

Unlike the delinquent group which utilizes the Internet café for games and as a gathering place, the gang members involved in credit card fraud use the Internet café and public libraries to obtain Internet access. Two younger generation members identified a specific older generation Chinese gang member who gathers credit card numbers and names of the credit card holders. The Chinese member obviously leads the credit card scheme and recruits younger generation members through Sonny. As Matt says, " I saw many times Zap with a stack of credit card receipts in his pocket or in a brown paper bag." Matt also advised that upon receipt of the fraudulently purchased packages, he (Zap) would then fence them off through electronic storefront locations in the New York City area. The managers of these storefront locations would usually pay 40 percent of the retail value of the item. Overall, Matt estimates that he is netting about $1,000, while Zap is making about $3,000 a month.

Check Fraud

Check fraud is usually committed by older generation gang members with their girl friends, who are usually older than they are. However, younger generation members are also used to pilfer checks from mailboxes or to drive older generation members and their girlfriends out to stores or malls. As James said, "Fred (the other partner in the older generation) would hit up young people (younger generation members) and get them to steal boxes of checks from people's personal mailboxes." He continues, "Now, although Fred went out with us sometimes, he never went into any of the stores. He never wanted to risk it. But other times, we would have someone (usually a younger generation member) who just did the driving."

Although James used to work in the credit card fraud, he was only engaged in check fraud at the time of the interview. When he was asked the reason he was only involved in check fraud, instead of credit card fraud, he explained:

Well, first of all, I prefer check fraud over credit card fraud. The reason being is when you have stolen credit cards, the verification process the store uses with the credit card companies happens too quickly. More chances to burn you. With stolen checks on the other hand, the victim wouldn't know their checks were stolen until weeks later, or at least thirty days later when they got their statements. So you had time to play with. Plus, with credit cards you really should know the victim's social security number.

After successfully obtaining the checks, they look at the checkbooks and see what types of checks were there. He continues, "What you want to see is the check numbers. If you get check numbers that are in a series of 1000 or below, it'll run you about $150 to $200. With check numbers in a series between 1000 to 3000, that will run you $300. But if you get checks that are 3000 and higher, they run you on average $500. These are the checks you want, 'cause higher check numbers are less suspicious." After obtaining the fraudulent checks, James would then proceed to obtain a fraudulent identification card bearing the victim's name and other details. However, prior to making any I.D., James or his girlfriend would proceed to a photo shop and get a passport photo of himself or herself, since they were going to be the runners who were going to impersonate the victims. They would then provide the photos to Fred who would then turn them over to a contact who would make the I.D. Upon obtaining the completed false identification cards, they were then required to memorize the information, in case they were asked any spontaneous questions by any retail employees. They usually pick weekends for the check fraud. As James says, "Fridays, Saturdays, and Sundays. Those are the good days, 'cause on Fridays and Saturdays, stores are so busy, the cashiers wouldn't pay much attention to you. So they just push you out of there. But Sundays stores are so slow they are just dying for business, so they always welcome you."

Like credit card fraud, the types of merchandise they bought through check fraud are electronics such as laptop computers and palm pilots. The areas or stores where they fence the items are also located in New York City. As James describes,

It was electronics, like laptop computers or palm pilots. Hitachi Laptops were hot. Tools were also really big. You can get tools and then fence them off to the local stores. Otherwise, most of the electronic stuff we fenced off were to stores in New York City. The specific areas there were around 8th and 38th streets. Another store was located right off 42nd Street. The owners of the stores were Arabic. They would usually give you 40 to 50 percent of whatever the retail price was of the item you were fencing.

Escort Service

None of the six members who participated in the study actually takes part in the escort service. Therefore, the description here is based on the knowledge of a younger generation member, Willie. A group of gang members with escort service girls teams up to run the business. They advertise the escort service in local newspapers. Either an older generation member or an escort service girl is always there to answer the phones and maintain all the escorts' schedules. Again, there are different roles for older generation and younger generation members as in other non-traditional gang activities. The role of younger generation members is usually to drive the girls off to the sites where the clients stay. The younger generation members are driving around the site until the girl(s) are come out. Sometimes, they have to face a conflict situation between clients and escort service girls. In such a situation, it is extremely rare for them to use any violence toward the clients because they don't want to have any attention from law enforcement. Instead, they are told to solve the problem in favor of the clients such as changing girls, providing services as they requested, or renegotiating the escort fees, which range from about $200 to $400 an hour.

Escort service girls used to work in massage parlors or as hostesses who were employed to entertain guests in Korean bars. Of the adult types of escort service such as exotic dancing, strip teasing, or lingerie modeling, the main service they provide is the erotic massage with sex, which is illegal. For that reason, the "receptionist" who gets an escort service call is cautious when asked anything regarding the escort service, in case the caller is a law enforcement officer. Even escort service girls are trained regarding this matter before they provide their services. For example, they may ask the client to take off his pants, possibly even play with himself before they will do anything.

Other Gang Activities

As previously described, traditional extortion is not available today. As James says, "You don't see a lot extorting or being extorted." Instead, they are partnerships with business owners. Recall Tae Ho, the leader of one section of the Korean Power gang. His role was managing the Korean pub as a general manager. Then, he claimed that he hired his members as guards, and so they are paid. Like the Korean Power gang, the Mo Ming Pai gang also utilizes a similar method of involvement in the bar or club industry. As Matt describes, "They (older generation brothers) have connections where a few bars and clubs they provide protection to actually manage and share the money." Compared to the Korean Power gang, the Mo Ming Pai gang seems to have less degree of responsibility for managing the bars and clubs. This also results in two operational differences in managing the clubs. First, they may not require much of a work force to take care of the business unless the business has ongoing problems. Therefore, it is not necessary for them to hire the younger generation members as guards on a regular basis. Second, there is no female business manager, like Tae Ho's girlfriend who recruits waiters, chefs, and other helpers because the actual management is usually done by owners or by someone hired by the owners.

The older generation members are also engaged in illegal gambling operations. In addition to the statement that was provided earlier from the member who got arrested while he worked as a gambling debt collector, the following conversation illustrates the operation.

KS: What else do they (older generation) do?

Matt: That's pretty much about it. Oh.... yeah. There was one time, one of the older generation (members) asked me to be a bouncer at a gambling joint, you know, illegal gambling place. They asked me if I wanted to have a job. I said "no" because I didn't want to spend around like five or seven hours doing nothing because I didn't need money.

KS: What do you mean do nothing?

Matt: Basically, you do nothing. You just walk around like you know... There are people watching things, you know, what's going on. Anybody cheating or, you know, is anybody here we'd call trouble, you know. Basically, you just walk around and watch people, make sure there's no trouble among people. If there is, break it up, you break it apart. Take them outside, whatever. You just take care of everything. You make sure everything is running smooth, you know. You just do nothing, you know.

KS: Have you been there?

Matt: Yeah, two or three times.

Younger generation members who are not involved in the group criminal activities emphasize their interest in brotherhood in the Mo Ming Pai, rather than in money-generating activities. As a result, they tend to commit individually-oriented crimes. For example, Matt says, "I never thought about making money in the gang other than just selling drugs on my own or mugging kind of on my own. That was more than enough to me." Overall, the analysis of the group activities shows that the gang activities are quite different from the delinquent group's. It also shows that there are different activity patterns within the gang, which clearly distinguish between generations. Activities such as drug selling and mugging are done by individual younger generation members, while those such as credit card fraud and escort services are done by a small subgroup of the gangs, rather than a whole gang.

CHAPTER 8
Conclusion

What is a gang or not is still a battle among many scholars. To avoid issues about fundamental definitions, this study adopted as an operational definition the "self-claim method." The reason behind this methodology was, "Let them define who they are because they know themselves better than anyone else." However, before the subjects identified themselves either as a gang or not, they took either one of two types of identity adaptation through the acculturation process, the Fobbies and Twinkies, which had already occurred to second-generation Koreans. Their identity gained through acculturation directly led these Korean youths to form or join delinquent groups or gangs. As seen in the previous chapters, the delinquent group and the gang differed in structure, process, and, particularly, in group activities. It is now time to consider the theoretical implications of the Korean American group delinquency.

THEORETICAL IMPLICATION

It is important to examine the immigration processes of both the first- and second-generation Koreans together, because the immigration process the first generation undergoes often relates to the next generation's group delinquency problem. In a larger sense, "deindustrialization" has affected Korean immigrants as it did the general population of the United States. Before the "deindustrialization" phenomenon swept America, well-paid manufacturing jobs allowed many immigrants to achieve the American dream. Today, immigrants constantly migrate with their American dreams to metropolitan areas in the United States, but the U.S. economy in the era of global economic restructuring generates almost no meaningful jobs for these new immigrants.

Figure 2 Korean Acculturation Process and Group Delinquency

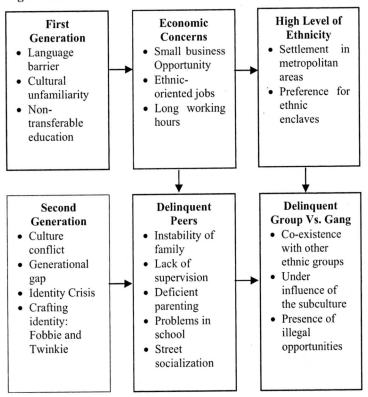

To overcome this economic situation, along with other difficulties such as the language barrier, cultural unfamiliarity, and non-transferable educational credentials, a large portion of Korean immigrants open small businesses in urban inner cities and work for long hours. In addition, due to a high level of ethnicity, most Koreans prefer to settle in ethnic enclaves where they enjoy their customs, and engage in ethnic-related jobs that normally do not require English. This settlement pattern and hard-work ethic among the first generation Korean immigrants somehow backfires with the second-generation Koreans.

Existing literature downplays the importance of how acculturation identity integrates into group context. As figure 2 illustrates, young Koreans go through the immigration process as the first or older generation does. However, their experience is quite different. While their parents have severe language problems, they usually do not have a similar language problem. While their parents adhere to a high level of Korean ethnicity, young Koreans often are confused about who they are: am I American, or Korean? This identity crisis often leads most young Koreans to craft their identities as either Fobbies or Twinkies, based on their level of acculturation. Regardless of their identity, they absorb American values and norms quicker than their parents. This high level of Americanization compared to their parents leads to a widened generational gap between themselves and their parents. Since the generation gap is a universal phenomenon among U.S. families, it should be considered as a precondition to deficient parenting, which escalates with a lack of parental supervision due to long working hours. These long working hours are inevitable for many Korean parents as they are immigrants who have to face economic concerns, resulting in opening small businesses where both parents are working with a minimum number of employees to save labor expenses. For this reason, many participants in the study are economically stable families, although some are below the poverty line in terms of family income. Therefore, deficient parenting, which is caused by a lack of supervision as a consequence of long working hours, and a generation gap born out of cultural conflict, play important roles in shaping Korean delinquent peers in schools or streets, along the lines of acculturation identity rather than poverty or other family problems identified with other ethnic gangs. The other thing that must be noticed is that before a group of young Koreans develops into a delinquent group or joins a gang, they are more likely to start with a small number of delinquent peers. This phenomenon, the most common type of delinquent group in which juvenile offenses are committed, is the small companionship group, consisting of two or three boys, has been observed in many studies. Recall that both the delinquent group in Palisades Park and the third generation of the Mo Ming Pai gang in Flushing began with three or four school friends who committed delinquent activities as a group. Depending on the type of crime, a small number of members' criminal engagements continue after their joining the gang or delinquent group.

Again, the economic concerns among the first-generation Korean immigrants create the settlement pattern in metropolitan areas. At the same time, the high level of ethnicity directs them to Korean ethnic enclaves where other minority ethnic groups often coexist. These settlements also may determine delinquent peers' development into a delinquent group or Korean gang or Chinese gang. As seen in chapter 4, the two research sites of Korean communities are different in many ways. These different characteristics of the communities accompany different types of Korean delinquent- related groups. While delinquent groups, Korean gangs, and Korean-affiliated Chinese gangs are found in the Chinese-dominated community, only delinquent groups are present in the Korean-dominated community. While the delinquent groups in the Korean-dominated community seem to emerge and die out in a relatively short time period, the gangs in the Chinese-dominated community survive through new membership generations. Moreover, the delinquent groups in the Chinese- dominated community have a great potential to develop into gangs. The study also found the delinquent groups and the gangs differed not only in their claims of gang identification, but also in their major activities. These major differences between these groups in both communities actually resulted from the level of exposure to other ethnic groups' subcultures and their influence on Korean youths' different acculturation identities.

The previous chapters indicate that types of activities also differ for delinquent groups, Korean gangs, and Chinese gangs. The difference in gang activities is found in the generations within the gang. The younger generation's motive is more about belonging, fun, or brotherhood, while the older generation's motive is more about money-generating illegal businesses. When the members of the younger generation participate in the money-generating business, their roles are often limited to provide support. As described earlier, this circumstance occurs when a small number of individuals in the group, rather than the group as a whole, engage in different types of illegal activities. These inter- and intra- group differences are also explained by the opportunity structure in the community. As a member describes,

In a sense, opportunity-wise, group activity (is) dictated by opportunity. I mean (the) group can't sell drugs unless you have a drug connection. Right now, the most popular activity is illegal immigrant smuggling. Just say a Korean group, they're not exposed this kind of activity because opportunity is not there...To the Asian community, the rackets or vices are very limited. All the forms of illegal activities in the community are robbery, burglary, drug, extortion, illegal smuggling. These are the main forms of criminal activity that'is available. But when you talk about drugs, you don't have a big market, so you might have individual kids coming out and selling a small amount of drugs. Extortion, it's not there anymore. So a lot of groups are not involved in extortion. Illegal human smuggling, it's not available to these kids.

Nevertheless, the nature of the delinquent group or gang often creates a deviant environment and opportunities. For instance, status delinquencies at the parties, such as heavy drinking, illicit substance abuse or fighting, would not likely happen if an individual were not with a group of peers. Mugging and robberies would not likely happen if the gang or the delinquent group did not maintain itself through recreational activities such as fun and unity. As discussed earlier, fun or other recreational activities happen after young members' association with these groups, which provide group maintenance and support. Staying longer in the gang or the delinquent group also drives older members to seek out alternative illegal opportunities, such as non-traditional crimes, as seen in the Mo Ming Pai gang's involvement in escort services, credit card fraud, or check fraud, as the number of other illegal opportunities available to these groups in the community become scarce. Therefore, if we assume that illegal opportunities are present everywhere, the study of the types of delinquent groups and youth gangs and their characteristics are keys to understanding them.

What has been said so far in this section carries with it the assumption that the analysis made here of types of acculturation identity and types of delinquent related groups will be found useful in the study of other immigrant groups. The principal support for this assumption lies in the fact that parallel types of identities and youth groups are found in analyzing the responses of subjects who experience the immigration process in metropolitan ethnic enclaves in the United

States. In other words, categories that fit the behavior of children of Korean immigrants in relation to their peers in daily life, can most likely be applied to other examples of human behavior. However, the conceptual models that will give a really good fit to the complexities of group behavior among immigrants need further work. Methods must be developed, data must be gathered, but most of all, systematic thinking must be done before such models can be built. Meanwhile, the present work may reinforce the presumption that basic patterns of youth group structure, process, and behavior will appear either as parts of these models, or as parts of a master tool.

POLICY IMPLICATION

A number of policy implications are suggested by the conclusions of this study. One point that should be perfectly clear is that the special problem of adjusting to the American scene is not one that confronts the first generation immigrants alone. Problems of adjustment certainly affect their children too. The second generation encounters conflicting cultural norms to an even greater extent than their parents. The status of immigrant minority groups has in itself such an importance for the adjustment of the second generation as to provide grounds for expecting that the third and fourth generations, even if removed from contact with an alien culture, will still have problems deriving from their nationality origin. Social workers and others who have practical experience with various immigrant groups are already well aware of these facts.

However, current programs for new Korean immigrants are often designed for targeting their clients separately, either the first generation or second generation only. Moreover, there is a lack of cooperation among these social agencies in Korean communities. Although it is best to establish a program to coordinate services for meeting the needs of the Korean immigrants in general and to formulate a strategy to address comprehensive issues regarding youths at risk, delinquent peers, delinquent groups, Korean gangs, and Chinese gangs, utilizing the existing agencies is the most efficient option. The objective of this program is to create networks among them and coordinate their efforts with one another. Three different networking systems should be implemented. First, different social agencies in a Korean community should cooperate. Second, agencies in the New Jersey Korean community should work together with those in New York. Last, agency networking should also extend to interethnic agency coordination between Korean social agencies and Chinese agencies. The major obstacle to implementing these networks is conflicts of interest among agencies, because their goals and target clients are different.

Compared to other ethnic communities, one of the remarkable characteristics of the Korean community is religious resources. As described earlier, they have provided not only spiritual fellowship, but also ethnic camaraderie, cultural identity, and social services. According to the 2000 Korea Time Business Directory, more than four hundred religious churches are registered in Queens and Bergen counties. Out of these, about 95 percent are Protestant and more than 40 percent of these churches are concentrated in Flushing. They are, by far, the most popular and most important to Korean immigrants, regardless of gender, age, economic status, whether a newcomer or an old-timer in the U.S. As long as the Korean churches provide the needs of Korean immigrants, their role will constantly increase in the future.

Table 13 Korean Religious Churches				
Types of churches	Queens	Flushing	Bergen	Palisades Park
Protestant	276	108	109	6
Catholic	2	1	2	0
Buddhist (Temples)	10	7	2	0
Total	288	116	113	6
Source: 2000 *Korea Time Business Directory*				

Since some participants in this study mentioned maturing and religious conversion as reasons to break away from the gangs, the most effective control agency for the social program would be through these religious institutions, which have obviously initiated many current community programs focusing on Korean youth and gang prevention. However, these programs face many difficulties in reaching out to those who need help, due to the misconceptions of parents and youths about these programs being insipid. Therefore, these programs must be a part of a networking system to reorganize and train staff to provide services to parents and their children.

A point about which few people who have practical experience with the second generation may also be aware is the diversity of delinquent-related groups. For example, a gang is just one of many forms of delinquent groups, but not every delinquent group is a gang. It thus should be clear that agencies and programs that are trying to aid in the adjustment of the second generation cannot succeed by making simply a uniform approach to all these groups. Awareness of this group diversity is undoubtedly valuable, not only to the social worker in these community programs but to the policy makers, law enforcement personnel, and especially all who are concerned with assisting in the Americanization of immigrant groups. In the planning of any practical work designed to help these immigrant youth groups, their differences need urgently to be considered.

Notification Form

This study is being done in order to develop a substantive theory explaining the causation and formation of gangs and their dynamics among Korean youth. If you agree to be part of this study you will be interviewed to tell your experiences in everyday life and anything you think I ought to know.

The information you provide will be held strictly in confidence. An identification number will be used to denote the source of information that you provide. Instead of your name, pseudonyms will be used and any identifying characteristic will be removed in any research report. This consent form and other files containing confidential information about you will be kept in a secured place at the investigator's house. These materials will be destroyed after the study is completed.

By participating in this study, there are no known risks to you. Participation in this study is up to you. There will be no penalty if you not participate in the study or if you decide to withdraw from it at any time. Your participation in this study is highly appreciated because the study is about people like you and it is important to let others know who you are and what you have experienced.

If you have questions about the study, I will answer them at this time. If you have further questions later on, you can reach me at 973-353-5929.

Consent Form

Pseudonym _____ voluntarily agree to participate in this study. He or she understands a copy of this consent form and notification will be received. As an appreciation of their participation on this study, they will receive 20 dollars after completing interview.

Identification Number_____Date_____

Social and Physical observation Instrument

1.   DATE_____NAME OF PLACE _____

2.   TIME OF OBSERVATION_____:_____ AM/PM

3.   PERIOD OF WEEK
     1=WEEK DAY
     2=WEEK NIGHT
     3=WEEKEND DAY
     4=WEEKEND NIGHT

4.   WEATHER CONDITION
     1=CLEAR
     2=PARTLY CLEAR
     3=CLOUDY
     4=RAIN

5.   NUMBER OF JUVENILES: MALE____FEMALE____

6.   EVENTS:
     1=DRUG
     2=DRINKING
     3=PHYSICAL ASSAULT
     4=LOUD NOISE/MUSIC
     5=VANDALISM
     6=OTHER

7.   PHYSICAL CONDITION:
     1=GRAFFITI (LITTLE/MODERATE/HEAVY)
     2=LITTER (LITTLE/MODERATE/HEAVY)
     3=BROKEN GALSS (LITTLE/MODERATE/HEAVY)
     4=OTHER (LITTLE/MODERATE/HEAVY)

8.   POLICE INTERACTION

Questions Used at Informal Interview

1. Please tell me about everyday life? (Ask routine activities of a typical day)

2. How do you like school? (If students, ask whether they like it or not/ if not students, ask why they stop schooling)

3. Please tell me about your friends? (What do these friends mean to your life? Ask separately about boyfriends and girlfriends)

4. Please tell me about your family life (What do you think about your parents? If any conflict, ask the cause of conflict)

5. Please tell me about gang life (If gang member, initial involvement, leadership, fighting, drugs, the number of gang member etc/ if not gang member, ask whether they heard about gangs)

6. What do you know about Korea or America? What do you call yourself? Korean? Korean-American? American?

7. Finally, would you like to say something else that you think I need to know to study Korean-American juveniles?

Formal Questionnaire

GENERAL INFORMATION

1. Where were you born?
    1) Korea
    2) United States
    3) Other (specify)_____
    4) Not Sure

2. How many family members do you have including you? Number of persons_____

3. What year did you begin living in the United States? Year 19____Not Sure_____

4. How old are you now?_____Year-old

5. What is your current marital status?
    1) Single
    2) Living as married
    3) Married
    4) Other (specify)_____
    5) Not sure

6. What was the highest grade of school that you have completed?
    1) No formal schooling
    2) 6th grade or less
    3) 7th to 9th grade
    4) 10th to 12th grades or GED
    5) College or graduate school
    6) Not sure

7. How well do you speak, read, and write English?

	Very Well	Somewhat Well	Average	Poor	Very Poor
Speak	5	4	3	2	1
Read	5	4	3	2	1
Write	5	4	3	2	1

8. Do you have a legitimate job?
    1) Yes, full time
    2) Yes, part time
    3) No
    4) No, full time student
    5) Don't know

9. If you are working full or part-time, what is your occupation?
   Subject's occupation: _____

10. What year did you parents begin living in the United States?
    Your mother: year 19____
    99) Born in America
    88) Not sure
    Your father: year 19_____
    99) Born in America
    88) Not sure

11. What do your parents do for a living? (If more than one job, indicate the job they more often involved in)
    Mother's occupation: _____
    Father's occupation: _____

12. What was the highest grade of school that your parents completed?
    Your mother: _____
    Your father: _____

SCHOOL

13. Are you currently enrolled in school?
     1)   Yes, full-time
     2)   Yes, part-time
     3)   No (skip to question #16)

14. Do you like school?
     1)   Yes
     2)   No
     3)   Don't know
What do you like/dislike most about school? (Probes: studying, learning, classmates, teachers, language problem, useless, boring)

15. How well are you doing in school?
     1)   Very well
     2)   Somewhat well
     3)   Not so well
     4)   Not well at all
     5)   Not sure
(Skip question #16 if subject is currently attending school)

16. Have you ever attended school since you arrived in the United States?
     1)   Yes
     2)   No
If yes, what caused you to stop attending school?

PARENTS AND HOMELIFE
17. Do you live at home with your parents most of the time?
     1)   Yes
     2)   No
If no, where else do you stay when you don't stay at home?

18. How often do you talk to or see your parents?
     1)   Always
     2)   Often
     3)   Sometimes
     4)   Rarely

19. How well do you get along with your parents?
    1) Very well
    2) Well enough
    3) Not quite well
    4) Not well at all
    5) Don't know

20. How much of the time do you think your parents understand you?
    1) Never
    2) Once in a while
    3) Often
    4) Most of the time
    5) All of the time
    6) Don't know

FRIENDS

21. How many of your friends are attending school?
    1) All
    2) Most
    3) Some
    4) A few
    5) None
    6) Don't know

22. How many of your friends belong to a gang?
    1) All
    2) Most
    3) Some
    4) Few
    5) None
    6) Don't know

GANG/ DELINQUENT GROUP

23. Are you currently a member of a gang?
    1) Yes (Which gang or group: _____)?
    2) No

If no, were you a member of a gang or delinquent group before? (Former peripheral member?)
     1)   Yes (Which gang or group: _____)?
     2)   No

If no, are you a peripheral member of a gang?
     1) Yes (Which gang: _____)?
     2) No

If no, are you associating with gang members occasionally or asked to join a gang and give it serious consideration?
     1) Yes (Which gang: _____)
     2) No (if no, stop the interview, the subject should not be included in the study)

SOCIAL PROCESSES OF JOINING AND DISSOCIATING A GANG

24. How old were you when you first joined (associated with) a gang (gang members)? Age: _____year-old

25. Before you joined a gang, did you hang out with gang members?
     1) Yes, the same gang
     2) Yes, but other gang (Specify: _____)

26. Why did you join a gang? (Probes: friendship; identity; power; money; forced to join; girls; fun; excitement; self-protection)

27. Tell me the processes of how you became a "member" (i.e. who introduced you? under what circumstances? did you have to take oaths? was there a formal or informal initiating ceremony?)

28. What did you know about gangs before you joined? (What do you know about gangs that you are associating with?)

29. After you joined the gang, how did you feel about being a gang member?

30. Before you joined (associated with) the gang, how often were you involved in any of the following activities?

	Never	Rarely	Sometimes	Often
Fighting	1	2	3	4
Stealing	1	2	3	4
Gambling	1	2	3	4
Asking money from stores	1	2	3	4
Asking money from pedestrians	1	2	3	4
Refusing to pay for food	1	2	3	4
Using drugs	1	2	3	4
Carrying a weapon	1	2	3	4

31. Did you encounter any problems in doing so?
    1) Yes
    2) No
If yes, what kinds of difficulties did you encounter? (Probes: the leader would not let me go; being harassed by other members; being threatened)

(For former gang members, ask the following question)
32. How long ago did you leave the gang?
    _____ Year(s) and _____ month(s) ago

33. Why did you decide to dissociate yourself form the gang?(Probes: too dangerous; did not worth it; did not want to disgrace family; found a good job; married; forced out by the gang; getting old)

34. How did you mange to drop out from the gang? (Probes: just stayed away; moved away; declared your intention to others)

35. Did you encounter any problems in doing so?
    1) Yes
    2) No
If yes, what kinds of difficulties did you encounter? (Probes: the leader would not let me go; being harassed by other members; being threatened)

GANG STRUCTURE AND DYNAMICS

36. On the average, how many members are there in your gang at any given time?
    1) Number of core members: _____
    2) Number of peripheral members, if any_____
    3) Not sure

37. How many gang members actively involved in the following activities?

	Most	Some	Few
Extortion	3	2	1
Fighting	3	2	1
Gambling	3	2	1
Drug Use	3	2	1
Drug Selling	3	2	1
Guarding the Street	3	2	1

38. How is your gang organized? (Probes: Are there gang leaders? How many types of leaders? How many types of followers?)

39. In your gang, is there a division of labor? That is, do gang members play different roles?
    1) Yes
    2) No
    If yes, how? (Probes: shooter; intimidator; guard; gun carrier; accountant; money collector; strategist)

40. How often do gang members in your gang get together?
    1) Almost everyday
    2) A few times a week
    3) Once a week
    4) Every tow week
    5) Once a month
    6) Once or twice a month
    7) A few times a year
    8) Don't know

41. In general, haw many people get together at any one time?_____ Number of people

42. What do gang members do when they get together? (Circles as many as possible)
    1) Just hang out
    2) Talk about gang business
    3) Go asking money from business owners
    4) Gamble
    5) Use drugs
    6) Eat
    7) Fight
    8) Any other reasons (Specify: _____)

43. How do members in your gang get along?
    1) Very well
    2) Well enough
    3) Not so well
    4) Not well at all
    If answer is 3) or 4), why do you say so? (Probes: Is there any fractions within the gang? Any problem with the ways money was distributed. Are members assaulted each other?)

44. As far as you know, how were followers promoted to leader? (Probes: smart; aggressive; leadership; loyalty; good connection; good relationship with the community; do time)

45. Are there rules for gang members?
    1) Yes
    2) No
    If yes, what are these rules? Who makes the rules?

46. What happens to gang members who break the rules?

47. In your opinion, how well organized is your gang?
    1) Very well-organized
    2) Somewhat organized
    3) Not organized at all
    4) Not sure
    Why do you say so?

48. Does your gang have places to hangout?
    1) Yes
    2) No
    If yes, were and what kind of places are they?

49. Does your gang have a specific territory?
    1) Yes
    2) No
    If yes, which areas your gang control?

50. Does your gang have branches or splinter groups in other cities in the United States?
    1) Yes
    2) No
    If yes, how is your group here related to those groups in other cities? (Probes: assist each other in times of crises; work together; visit each other's place often; talk to each other; provide refuge)

GANG ACTIVITIES
51. Describe a typical day, starting when you get up in the morning

52. In the past year, how often have you been involved in the following activities?

	Daily	Wkly	Mty	A Few	1 or 2	None
Asking protection money regularly	5	4	3	2	1	0
Asking protection money irregularly	5	4	3	2	1	0
Asking money from pedestrians	5	4	3	2	1	0
Taking money from business owners	5	4	3	2	1	0
Selling items to business owners	5	4	3	2	1	0
Eating for free	5	4	3	2	1	0
Beat someone	5	4	3	2	1	0
Shoot someone	5	4	3	2	1	0
Break into houses to rob	5	4	3	2	1	0

53. Other than the above-mentioned activities, what types of other illegal activities are you involved in?

54. In the past year, how much money did you and your gang earn from the following activities?

	You	Your Gang
Protection and extortion		
Selling items		
Guarding the gambling places		
Selling drugs		
Other (Specify: _____)		

GANG VIOLENCE

55. Have you ever taken part in fights with members of other gangs?
    1) Yes
    2) No
    If yes, please explain the latest such incident?

56. What are the causes of conflicts among various gangs?

57. How do these intergangs fights typically happen? (Probes: are weapons used; where do they take place; who participate)

58. When there are conflicts or tensions among gangs, are there peaceful ways to solve the conflicts?
    1) Yes
    2) No
    If yes, how?

59. Have you ever taken part in fights with members of your own gang?
    1) Yes
    2) No
    If yes, please explain the latest such incident?

60. What are the causes of conflicts among members of your gang?

61. How does these intragang fights typically happen? (Probe: are weapons used; where do they take place; who participate)
62. When there are conflicts or tensions among members of the same gang, are there peaceful ways to solve the conflicts?
    1) Yes
    2) No
    If yes, How?

DRUG USE AND ARREST

63. How often have you used the following drugs in the past year?

	Almost Daily	Almost Weekly	Almost Monthly	A Few Times	Once or Twice	None
Alcohol	5	4	3	2	1	0
Marijuana	5	4	3	2	1	0
Crack	5	4	3	2	1	0
Cocaine	5	4	3	2	1	0
Heroin	5	4	3	2	1	0
Other (_____)	5	4	3	2	1	0

64. Do you sell drugs or help others sell drugs?
    1) Yes
    2) No
    If yes, describe your drug selling activities. How much did you earn this way in the past year?

65. How many times have you been arrested?
    _____ Number of arrests

66. If ever arrested, describe the last time when you were arrested? What were the charges?

67. Have you ever been to jail or prison?
    1) Yes
    2) No
    If yes, describe the last incident? What were the charges?

GENERAL OPINIONS

68. In your opinions, why are Korean-American gangs growing   in Korean community?

69. Now that we have completed the interview, do you have any comments or questions?

70. In case I wish to get further information from you in the future, are you willing to be interviewed again?

Profile of the Delinquent Group Members

Name	General Information (In 2000)	Family and Home Life	Education and School life	Education and School life
Joong	• Age: 18 • Immigration: 1992 • Level of English: Average	• Parents: divorce • Father: small business-garment • Mother: lives in Korea alone • Older brother, Dongbin • Since 1997, living only with his older brother, Dongbin, in a small apartment • Contact and maintain good relation with his mother in Korea	• Average in academic performance • One year older than other students at the same grade • Notorious school experience such as suspension and detention due to his behavioral problems • Completed his high school diploma in 2001	• The first meeting through a billiard club manager • Physical appearance does not fit images of high school students: hair with tinges of red color • Good at pool games and owned his own cue stick • Work experience in a couple of Internet cafes

Name	General Information (in 2000)	Family and Home Life	Education and School life	Other Description
Manho	• Age: 18 • Immigration: 1990 • Level of English: Average	• Father: works in a Korean grocery store • Mother: works for Kunsun's nail salon • Older sister: attends an Ivy League university • Serious conflict with family members, but maintain good relation after dropout	• Many troubles in school • Expelled from school at 11th grade in the fall of 1998 • On his last day of school, damaged chairs and desks in a classroom in front of schoolteacher • Still had a grudge against the schoolteachers	• Joong's closest school friend before expelling • Part time job experience such as Karaoke, billiard club, or Internet café • Full time job at a deli store in Manhattan

Name	General Information (in 2000)	Family and Home Life	Education and School life	Other Description
Kunsun	• Age: 18 • Immigration: 1991 • Level of English: Average	• Father: passed away • Mother: small business-nail salon • Younger brother: Sungjin, who associates with the group a year later • Ran away couple of times • Get along with his mother, but had conflict with his young brother	• Attend a different neighborhood high school • Many behavioral problems in the school, engaging in fist fighting • Completed high school in 2000	• Physically bigger and stronger than his friends • Drives a luxury BMW sport car • Night shift work experience in an internet café with Joong and Manho, and part time at local cellular phone store after school

Name	General Information (in 2000)	Family and Home Life	Education and School life	Other Description
Dongbin	• Age: 20 • Immigration: 1992 • Level of English: Average	• Parents: divorce • Father: small business-garment • Mother: lives in Korea alone • Younger brother, Joong • Serious conflict with his parents regarding dropout of the school	• Stop schooling in 1997 because his belief of schooling is to make money but he did not see any good chance to make good money after school	• The time of his dropout from school is the same time period of his parents in the process of divorce • Work experience in Korean groceries and fish markets although he can work in his father's garment factory
Kangso	• Age: 20 • Immigration: 1991 • Level of English: Average	• Parents: small business • No further information regarding his family, except they moved from New Jersey to Bayside, New York after his dropout of high school	• Many believed his falsehood as a college student majoring criminal justice at John Jay college • Dropout at 12th grade • Took GED	• Through him, many members accessed street drugs such as marijuana and Ecstasy • Joined the army in the early spring of 2001

Name	General Information (in 2000)	Family and Home Life	Education and School life	Other Description
Sungjin	• Age: 16 • Immigration: 1991 • Level of English: Somewhat good	• Father: passed away • Mother: small business-nail salon • Older brother: Kunsun • Complaining but good relation with his mother, but had conflict with his older brother, Kunsun	• Poor in academic performance • No behavioral problems in school and maintain good relation with teachers	• Completely join the group after June 2000 • Violently fought with his brother a couple of times when he took his brother's BMW and stole his brother's Ecstasy
Saemin	• Age: 16 • Immigration: 1995 • Level of English: poor	• Father: taxi driver • Mother: waitress • Two younger sisters • Parents immigrated first, leaving him and two sisters with grandparents for 3 years in Korea • Get along with parents well enough	• Positive in school life although poor in academic performance except math and science • No behavioral problems in school and maintain good relation with teachers	• Sungjin's good school friend

Name	General Information (in 2000)	Family and Home Life	Education and School life	Other Description
Dojung	• Age: 17 • Immigration: 2000 • Level of English: very poor	• Father: passed away • Mother: work for a massage room run by his relative • Strong bond to his mother	• Unknown how he registered in public school • Began to fight from his second school day	• Illegally immigrated to America, crossing over Canadian border with other Koreans • Strong personality • Fighting as many as he could until he won • Returned to Korea after one-year stay in the U.S.
Namsoo	• Age: 17 • Immigration: 1988 • Level of English: very good	• Father: professional realtor • Mother: home • Only son • Hyunsoo's cousin • Get along with parents well enough	• Positive in schooling • Good academic performance • Good relation with teachers	• Known as psycho due to his fighting with a group of white students in school cafeteria during lunchtime in front of teachers • Joined the group after conflict with Dojung

Name	General Information (in 2000)	Family and Home Life	Education and School life	Other Description
Hyunsoo	• Age: 17 • Immigration: 1986 • Level of English: very good	• Father: private CPA • Mother: manager in an insurance company • Older brother: works in a security company in Manhattan • Namsoo's cousin • Get along with parents well enough	• Positive in schooling • Excellent academic performance, top five in every class • Good relation with teachers • Certificate of merit from the school	• Joined the group after conflict with Dojung
Majoong	• Age: 17 • Immigration: 1991 • Level of English: somewhat good	• Father: restaurant chief • Mother: sewer in a garment factory • Poor relation with parents due to his parents' high educational expectation	• Talented at sports • Positive in schooling • Good academic performance • Good relation with teachers	• Joined the group after conflict with Dojung
Eugene	• Age: 17 • Immigration: born in America • Level of English: very good	• Parent: small business-laundry • Three years old sister and grandmother	• Average in academic performance • No behavioral problems	• Unusual association with the group because his acculturation level • Joined the group after conflict with Dojung

Profile of the Mo Ming Pai Gang members

Name	General Information (In 2000)	Family and Home Life	Education and School Life	Other Description
James	• Age: 22 • Immigration: 1985 • Level of English: Somewhat good	• Parents: small business-deli Store • Old sister: married • Serious conflict with parents • Father used to beat him • Lives with other gang members	• Poor in academic performance • Conflict with teachers • Dropout at 9th grade • Preparing GED	• Second generation • Small physical appearance • Used to associate with various gangs including Korean Power gang • Works as car salesperson • Many close Chinese friends
Willie	• Age: 20 • Immigration: Born in the USA • Level of English: Very good	• Parents: small business-wig wholesale • Good relation with his parents	• Average in academic performance • Completed high school	• Third generation • Many close Chinese friends

Name	General Information (in 2000)	Family and Home Life	Education and School life	Other Description
Don	• Age: 19 • Immigration: 1990 • Level of English: Somewhat good	• Father: Korean restaurant manager • Mother: Cashier at Korean supermarket • Parents immigrated in 1986 and he and two younger brothers rejoin their parents two years later • Good relation with his parents	• Average in academic performance • Conflict with other ethnic schoolmates • Completion of high school	• Third generation • No work experience • Became the best friend with Willie after joining the gang
Hana	• Age: 19 • Immigration: 1990 • Level of English: Very good	• Parents: small business-handbag and cap wholesale • Parents immigrated in 1989 and he rejoined their parents one year later • Somewhat good relation with his parents	• Average in academic performance • Completed high school	• Third generation • Used to associate with Korean Power gang members

Name	General Information (in 2000)	Family and Home Life	Education and School life	Other Description
Sam	• Age: 19 • Immigration: 1988 • Level of English: Very good	• Parents: separated • Father: handyman in Los Angeles area • Mother: various part time jobs • Get along with his mother good enough	• Average in academic performance • Completed high school	• Third generation
Matt	• Age: 17 • Immigration: Born in USA • Level of English: Very good	• Parents: small business-garment • Conflict with parents	• poor in academic performance • Dropout at 10th grade • Completed high school	• The fourth generation • Ex-Korean Power gang member • No work experience

Reference

Anderson, E. (1999). *Code of the Street*. New York: W. W Norton & Co.

Asbury, H. (1927). *Gangs of New York: An Informal History of the Underworld*. New York: Alfred A. Knopf, Inc.

Battin-Pearson, S. R., Thornberry, T., Hawkins, J. D., & Krohn, M. (1998). *Gang Membership, Delinquent Peers, and Delinquent Behavior*. Washington, D.C., Office of Juvenile Justice and Delinquency Prevention.

Blumstein, A. (2002). Youth, Guns, and Violent Crime. *The Future of Children, 12*(2), 39-53.

Bureau of Justice Assistance. (1993). *A Police Guide to Surveying Citizens and Their Environment*. Washington, D.C.: U.S. Government Printing Office.

Bursik, R. J., Jr., & Grasmick, H. G. (1993). *Neighborhoods and Crime: The Dimensions of Effective Community Control*. New York: Lexington Books.

Burtcher, K. F., & Piehl, A. M. (1998). Cross-City Evidence on the Relationship Between Immigration and Crime. *Journal of Policy Analysis and Management, 17*(3). 457-493.

Campbell, A. (1990). Female Participation in Gangs. In C. R. Huff (Ed.), *Gangs in America* (pp. 163-182). Thousand Oaks, CA: Sage Publications

Chea, K. M. (1990). *Korean-American Juvenile Delinquency in Relation to Acculturation Differences between Parents and Children*. Ph.D. Dissertation, Illinois Institute of Technology.

Chesney-Lind, M., Sheldon, R. G., & Joe, K. A. (1996). Girls, delinquency, and gang membership. In C. R. Huff (Ed.), *Gangs in America* (pp. 185-204, 2nd Ed.). Thousand Oaks, CA: Sage Publications

Chin, K. (1990). *Chinese subculture & criminality: Non-traditional crime groups in America*. Westport, CT: Greenwood.

Chin, K. (1996). *Chinatown Gangs*. New York: Oxford University Press

Claffey, M. (2001, May 24). 4 busted in Queens in savage gang attack. *Daily News*. Retrieved November 02, 2002, from http://web.lexis-nexis.com/universe

Cloward, R., & Ohlin. L. (1960). *Delinquency and Opportunity*. New York: The Free Press.

Cohen, A. (1955). *Delinquent Boys*. New York: The Free Press.

Curry, G. D., & Spergel, I. A. (1988). Gang Homicide, Delinquency, and Community. *Criminology, 26*(3), 381-405.

Curry, G. D., & Spergel, I. A. (1993). Gang Involvement and Delinquency among Hispanic and African American Adolescent Males. *Journal of Research in Crime and Delinquency, 29*, 273-291.

Decker, S., & Winkle, B.V. (1996). *Life in the Gang*. Cambridge, England: Cambridge University Press.

Doyle, J., & Khandelwal, M. (1997). *Ethnic Groups in the USA with over 100,000 Populations*. Retrieved November 22, 2001 from http://www.pff.net/Resources/ethnicusa.htm

Eghigian, M. & Kirby, K. (2006). Girls in Gangs: On the Rise in America. *Corrections Today, 68*(2). 48-50.

Egley, A. (2005). *Highlights of the 2002-2003 National Youth Gang Survey*. Washington, DC: U.S. Department of Justice, Office of Justice Programs, Office of Juvenile Justice and Delinquency Prevention

Egley, A., & Arjunan, M. (2002). *Highlights of the 200 National Youth Gang Survey*. Washington, DC: U.S. Department of Justice, Office of Justice Programs, Office of Juvenile Justice and Delinquency Prevention

English, T. J. (1995). *Born to Kill: America's Most Notorious Vietnamese Gang, and the Changing Face of Organized Crime*. New York: William Morrow and Company, Inc.

Erickson, M. L., & Jensen, G. F. (1977). Delinquency is Still Group Behavior! Toward Revitalizing the Group Premise in the Sociology of Deviance. *The Journal of Criminal Law and Criminology, 68*(2), 262-273.

Esbensen, F-A., & Huizinga, D. (1993). Gangs, drugs, and delinquency in a survey of urban youth. *Criminology, 31*, 565-589.

Fagan, J. (1989). The social organization of drug use and drug dealing among urban gangs. *Criminology, 27*(4), 663-67.

Fagan, J. (1990). Social Processes of Delinquency and Drug Use among Urban Gangs. In C. R. Huff (Ed.), *Gangs in America* (pp. 183-222). Thousand Oaks, CA: Sage Publications.

Fagan, J. (1996). Gangs, Drugs, and Neighborhood Change. In C. R. Huff (2nd Ed.), *Gangs in America* (pp. 39-74). Thousand Oaks, CA: Sage Publications.

Fenner, A. (2001, January 12). Teens admit cabbie slay. *Daily News*, New York, p2.

Generational Conflict among Korean family in New York. (2003, February 02). *Han-Kook Daily News*, p B.4.

Grennan, S., Britz, M.T., Rush, J., & Barker, T. (2000). *Gangs: An International Approach*. Upper Saddle River, NJ: Prentice Hall.

Greiner, J. M. (1994). Use of Ratings by Trained Observers. In J. S. Wholey, H. P. Hatry, & K. E. Newcomer (Eds.), *Handbook of Practical Program Evaluation*. San Francisco: Jossey-Bass.

Hagedorn, J. (1990). Back in the Field Again: Gang Research in the Nineties. In C. R. Huff (Ed.), *Gangs in America* (pp. 240-262). Thousand Oaks, CA: Sage Publications.

Hagedorn, J. (1998). *People and Folks: Gangs, Crime, and the Underclass in a Rustbelt City* (2nd Ed.). Chicago: Lake View Press.

Hakkert, A. (1998). Group Delinquency in the Netherlands: Some findings from an exploratory study. International *Review of Law, Computers & Technology, 12*(3), 453-475.

Haskins, J. (1974). *Street Gangs. Yesterday and Today*. New York: Hastings House Publishers.

Horowitz, C. F. (2001). *An Examination of U.S. Immigration Policy and Serious Crime*. Washington DC: Center for Immigration Studies

Howell, J. G. & Decker, S. H. (1999). *The Youth Gangs, Drugs, and Violence Connection*. Washington, DC: U.S. Department of Justice, Office of Justice Programs, Office of Juvenile Justice and Delinquency Prevention

Howell, J. G. & Egley, A. (2005). *Gangs in Small Towns and Rural Counties*. Washington, DC: U.S. Department of Justice, Office of Justice Programs, Office of Juvenile Justice and Delinquency Prevention

Huff, C. R. (1998). *Comparing the Criminal Behavior of Youth Gangs and At-Risk Youth*. Washington DC: National Institute of Justice

Hughes, L. A. & Short, J. F. Jr. (2005). Disputes Involving Youth Street Gang Members: Micro-Social Contexts. *Criminology, 45*(1). 43-76.

Huizinga, D. (1996). *The Influence of Delinquent Peers, Gangs, and Co-offending on Violence*. Washington, DC: Office of Juvenile Justice and Delinquency Prevention.

Hurh, W. M. (1998). *The New Americans: The Korean Americans*. Westport, CT: Greenwood Press.

Hurh, W. M., & Kim, K. C. (1984). *Korean Immigrants in America: A Structural Analysis of Ethnic Confinement and Adhesive Adaptation*. Rutherford, NJ.: Fairleigh Dickenson University Press.

Ianni, F. A. J. (1974). *Black Mafia: Ethnic Succession in Organized Crime*. New York: Simon & Schuster.

Immigration and Naturalization Service. (2003). *2001 Statistical Yearbook of the Immigration and Naturalization Service.* Washington, DC: U.S. Government Printing Office.

Inciardi, J. A. (1993). Some Consideration on the Methods, Dangers, and Ethics of Crack House Research. In J. A. Inciardi, D. Lockwood & A. E. Pettieger (Eds), *Women and Crack Cocaine,* (pp. 147-57). New York: Harper & Brothers.

Jackson, R. K., & McBride, W. D. (2000). *Understanding Street Gangs.* Incline Village, NV: Copperhouse Publishing Company.

Jankowski, M. S. (1991). *Islands in the Street: Gangs and American Urban Society.* Berkeley, CA: University of California Press.

Kershaw, S. (2001, July 5). Extortion Case Explores Rifts in Korean Enclave in Queens. *New York Times,* p. B1.

Kim, J. H. (1997). *Korean-American women and the Church.* Atlanta, GA: Scholars Press

Kim, S. S. (2001). *The Psychosocial Process of Negotiating Boundaries: A Grounded Theory of the Experiences of Young Korean Immigrants.* Ph.D. Dissertation, Rutgers University.

Klein, M. W. (1971). *Street gangs and street workers.* Englewood Cliffs, NJ: Prentice Hall.

Klein, M. W. (1995). *The American Street Gang: Its Nature, Prevalence, and Control.* New York: Oxford University Press.

Klein, M. W. & Maxson, C. L. (2001). *Gang Structures, Crime patterns, and Police Responses: A Summary Report.* Rockville, MD: National Criminal Justice reference Service.

Lee, J. S. (2004). *Intergenerational Conflict, Ethnic Identity and Their Influences on Problem Behaviors among Korean American Adolescents.* Ph.D. Dissertation. University of Pittsburgh.

Lee, S. R. (1988). *Self-concept correlates of Asian American cultural identity attitudes.* Ph.D. Dissertation, University of Maryland.

Lee, S. S. (1998). Personal communication. October 22.

Lee, Y. H. (1998). Acculturation and delinquent behavior: The case of Korean American youths. *International Journal of Comparative and Applied Criminal Justice, 22*(Fall), 273-293.

Leet, D. A., Rush, G. E., & Smith, A. M. (2000). *Gangs Graffiti and Violence.* Incline Village, NV: Copperhouse Publishing Company.

McCord, J. (1995). Ethnicity, Acculturation, and Opportunities: A Study of Two Generations. In D. F. Hawkins (Ed.), *Ethnicity, Race, and Crime: perspectives Across Time and Place* (pp. 69-81). Albany, NY: State University of New York Press.

Mangiafico, L. (1988). *Contemporary American Immigration: patterns of Filipino, Korean, and Chinese settlement in the United States.* New York, NY: Praeger.

Matsueda, R. L., & Anderson, K. (1998). The dynamics of delinquent peers and delinquent behavior. *Criminology, 36*, 269-308.

Maxfield, M. G., & Babbie, E. (1997). *Research Methods for Criminal Justice and Criminology* (2nd ed.). Belmont, CA: Wadsworth.

Maxson, C. L. (1998). Gang Members on the Move. *Juvenile Justice Bulletin*, October, 1-11. Washington, DC: Office of Juvenile Justice and Delinquency Prevention.

Maxson, C., & Klein, M. W. (1996). Defining gang homicide. In C. R. Huff (2nd Ed.), *Gangs in America* (pp. 3-20). Thousand Oaks, CA: Sage Publications.

Maxwell, J. A. (1996). *Qualitative Research Design: An Interactive Approach.* Thousand Oaks, CA: SAGE publications

Miller, J. (2001). *One of the Guys: Girls, Gangs and Gender.* New York: Oxford University.

Miller, W. B. (1958). Lower Class Culture as a Generating Milieu of Gang Delinquency. *Journal of Social Issues*, 14, 5-19.

Miller, W. B. (1975). *Violence by Youth Gangs and Youth Groups as a Crime Problem in Major American Cities.* Washington, D.C.: U.S. Government Printing Office.

Miller, W. B. (1982). *Crime by Youth Gangs and Groups in the United States.* Washington, D.C. : U.S. Department of Justice Programs, Office of Juvenile Justice and Delinquency Prevention (Reissued in 1992).

Miller, W. B. (2001). *The Growth of Youth Gang Problems in the United States: 1970-98.* Washington, D.C.: U.S. Department of Justice Programs, Office of Juvenile Justice and Delinquency Prevention.

Min, P. G. (1995). Korean Americans. In P. G. Min (Ed.), *Asian Americans: Contemporary Trends and Issues* (pp. 199-231). Thousand Oaks, CA: Sage Publications.

Min, P. G. (2006). Korean Americans. In P. G. Min (2nd Ed.), *Asian Americans: Contemporary Trends and Issues* (pp. 230-259). Thousand Oaks, CA: Sage Publications.

Moore, J. W. (1991). *Going Down to the Barrio.* Philadelphia: Temple University Press.

Moore, J. W., Vigil, J. D., & Garcia, R. (1983). Residence and Territoriality in Gangs. *Journal of Social Problems, 31*(2), 182-194.

National Youth Gang Center. (1997). *1995 National Youth Gang Survey.* Washington, DC: U.S. Department of Justice, Office of Justice Programs, Office of Juvenile Justice and Delinquency Prevention

National Youth Gang Center. (1998). *1996 National Youth Gang Survey.* Washington, DC: U.S. Department of Justice, Office of Justice Programs, Office of Juvenile Justice and Delinquency Prevention

National Youth Gang Center. (1999). *1997 National Youth Gang Survey.* Washington, DC: U.S. Department of Justice, Office of Justice Programs, Office of Juvenile Justice and Delinquency Prevention

National Youth Gang Center. (2000). *1998 National Youth Gang Survey.* Washington, DC: U.S. Department of Justice, Office of Justice Programs, Office of Juvenile Justice and Delinquency Prevention

New York City Youth Board. (1960). *Reaching the Fighting Gang.* New York: New York City Youth Board.

New York Korean Youth Center. (1998). *1997 Annual Report.* New York: Korean Youth Center of New York.

Oehme, C. G. III. (1997). *Gangs, Groups and Crime: Perceptions and Responses of Community Organizations.* Durham, NC: Carolina Academic Press

Office of the District Attorney (1992) *Gangs, Crime And Violence in Los Angeles: Findings and proposals from the District Attorney's Office.* Los Angeles, CA.

Oh, S. (1998). Korean-American college students: Multiple constructions of ethnic identity. *Dissertation Abstracts International, 58*(06), 2274. Retrieved October 21, 2001, from http://www.libraries.rutgers.edu/ovidweb.

Padilla, F. M. (1992). *The Gang as an American Enterprise.* New Brunswick, NJ: Rutgers University Press.

Park-Adams, J. (1997). The relationship between ethnic identity and psychological adjustment among Korean-Americans. *Dissertation Abstracts International, 58*(05), 2753B. Retrieved October 21, 2001, from http://www.libraries.rutgers.edu/ovidweb.

Park, E. J. K. (1995). Voices of Korean-American Students. *Adolescence, 30* (120), 945-53.

Pizarro, J. M. & McGloin, J. M. (2006). Explaining gang homicides in Newark, New Jersey: Collective behavior or social disorganization? *Journal of Criminal Justice, 34*(2). 195-207

Pogrebin, M. R., & Poole, E. D. (1990) Culture conflict and Crime in the Korean American Community. *Criminal Justice Policy Review, 4*(1), 69-78.

Portes, A. (1996). *The New Second Generation.* New York; Russell Sage.

Queens Chamber of Commerce. (1996). *Neighborhood Resources.* Retrieved December 11, 1988, from http://www.queenschamber.org/Queens/Neighborhood%20Pages/flushing.html

Reiss, A. J. Jr. (1988). Co-offending and Criminal Careers. *Crime and Justice: A Review of Research, 10*, 117-170.

Sanders, W. G. (1994). *Gangbangs and drive-bys: Grounded culture and juvenile gang violence.* New York: Aldine de Gruyter.

Sante, L. (1991). *Low life: Lures and snares of old New York.* New York: Farrar, Giroux and Straus.

Savada, A. M., & Shaw, W. (1990). *South Korea: A Country Report.* Library of Congress Retrieved December 11, 2001, from http://lcweb2.loc.gov/frd/cs/krtoc.html

Sellin, T. (1938). *Culture Conflict and Crime.* New York: Social Science Research Council.

Shaw, C. R., & McKay, H. D. (1942). *Juvenile Delinquency and Urban Areas.* Chicago: University of Chicago Press.

Shim, J. I. (1998). Personal communication. August 24.

Short, J. F. Jr. (1976). Gangs, Politics, and the Social Order. In J. F. Jr. Short (Ed.), *Delinquency, Crime and Society.* Chicago: University of Chicago Press.

Short, J. F. Jr. (1996). Personal, Gang, and Community Careers. In C. R. Huff (2nd Ed.), *Gangs in America* (pp. vii-xviii). Thousand Oaks, CA: Sage Publications.

Short, J. F. Jr. (1997). *Poverty, Ethnicity, and Violent Crime.* Boulder, CO: Westview Press.

Short, J. F. Jr., & Strodtbeck, F. L. (1965). *Group Process and Gang Delinquency.* Chicago: University of Chicago Press.

Song, J. H. L., Dombrink, J., & Geis, G. (1992) Lost in the Melting Pot: Asian Youth Gangs in the United States. *The Gang Journal, 1*(1), 1-13.

Spergel, I. A. (1995). *Youth Gang Problem.* Oxford, England: Oxford University Press.

Spradley, J. P. (1979). *The Ethnographic Interview.* New York: Harcourt Brace Jovanovich College Publishers.

Sullivan, M. L. (1989). *Getting Paid: Youth Crime And Work In The Inner City.* Ithaca. Cornell University Press.

Sullivan, M. L. (2000). *Gang Emergence in New York City: Continuity and Change in the Social Organization and Symbolic Representation of Youth Violence.* Working Draft. Newark, NJ: Rutgers University

Sung, B. L. (1977). *Gangs in New York Chinatown.* New York Department of Asian Studies, City College of New York, Monograph No.6

Sutherland, E. H., & Cressey, D. R. (1974). *Criminology* (9th ed.). Philadelphia: J.B. Lippincott.

Suttles, G. D. (1968). *The Social Order of the Slum.* Chicago: University of Chicago Press

Taylor, C. S. (1990). *Dangerous Society.* East Lansing, MI: Michigan State University Press.

Thornberry, T. P. (1998). Membership in Youth Gangs and Involvement in Serious and Violent Offending. In R. Loeber, R & D. P. Farrington (Eds.), *Serious and Violent Juvenile Offenders.* Thousand Oaks, CA: Sage Publication.

Thornberry, T. P., & Farnworth, M. (1983). Social Correlates of Criminal Involvement: Further Evidence on the Relationship between Social Status and Criminal Behavior. *American Sociological Review, 47*, 505-518.

Thornberry, T. P., Krohn, M. D., Lizotte, A. J., Smith, C. A., & Tobin, K. (2003). *Gangs and Delinquency in Developmental Perspective.* Cambridge, UK: Cambridge University Press

Thrasher, F. (1927). *The Gang: A study of 1313 gangs in Chicago.* Chicago: University of Chicago Press.

Tittle, C. R.,Villemez, W. J., & Smith, D. A. (1978). The Myth of Social Class and Criminality: An Empirical Assessment of the Empirical Evidence. *American Sociological Review, 43*, 643-656.

Tonry, M. (1997). Ethnicity, crime, and immigration. In M. Tonry (Ed.), *Crime and justice: A review of research,* 21, (pp. 2-18). Chicago: University of Chicago Press.

Toy, C. (1992) Coming Out to Play: Reasons to join and participate in Asian Gangs. *The Gang Journal, 1*(1), 13-29.

U.S. Bureau of the Census. (1993). *1990 Census of Population, Asian and Pacific Islanders in the United States (CP-3-5).* Washington, D.C.: U.S. Government Printing Office.

U.S. Bureau of the Census. (2000a). *Asian Population by Detailed Group:2000 (PCT5).* Washington, D.C.: U.S. Government Printing Office. Retrieved December 17, 2002, from http://www.census.gov/prod/2002pubs/c2kbr01-16.pdf.

U.S. Bureau of the Census. (2000b). *Asian Origins for Selected Groups.* Census 2000 Summary File 1 (SF1) 100 Percent Data, Table PCP5. Washington, D.C.: U.S. Government Printing Office. Retrieved December 17, 2002, from http://www.queenslibrary.org/pub/demographics_2000.asp?central= 0&branch=Flushing&page =3.

U.S. Bureau of the Census. (2000c). *Palisades Park borough, Bergen County, New Jersey.* Census 2000 Summary File 1 (SF1) Sample data, Table QT-P14. Washington, D.C.: U.S. Government Printing Office. Retrieved August 27, 2002, from http://factfinder.census.gov/servlet/QTTable? ds_name=D&geo-id=06000US3400355770&qr.

U.S. Federal News. (2006). *Two New York City Police Officers, Operators of Queens Brothel Charged in Bribery Scheme.* Washington: HT Media Ltd.

Vigil, J. D. (1988). *Barrio gangs: Street life and identity in Southern California.* Austin: University of Texas Press

Vigil, J. D. (1990). Cholos and gangs. In C. R. Huff (Ed.), *Gangs in America* (pp. 116-128). Thousand Oaks, CA: Sage Publications.

Vigil, J. D. (2003). Urban Violence and Street Gangs. *Annual Review of Anthropology, 32*, 225-42.

Vigil, J. D., & Yun, S. C. (1990). Vietnamese Youth Gangs in southern California. In C. R. Huff (Ed.), *Gangs in America* (pp. 146-162). Thousand Oaks, CA: Sage Publications.

Waters, T. (1999). *Crime and Immigrant Youth*. Thousand Oaks, CA: Sage Publications.

Warr, M. (1993). Age, Peers, and delinquency. *Criminology, 31*, 17-40

Warr, M. (1996). Organization and instigation in delinquent groups. *Criminology, 36*, 11-37

Whyte, W. F. (1943). *Street Corner Society*. Chicago: University of Chicago Press

Wilson, W. J. (1987). *The truly disadvantaged: The inner city, the underclass, and public policy*. Chicago: University of Chicago Press.

Wolfgang, M. E., & Ferracuti, F. (1967). *The Subculture of Violence-Towards an Integrated Theory in Criminology*. London: Tavistock Publications Ltd.

Wright, R., & Bennett, T. (1990). Exploring the Offender's Perspective: Observing and Interviewing Criminals. In K. L. Kempt (Ed.), *Measurement Issues in Criminology* (pp. 135-51). New York: Springer-Verlag.

Wright, R., Decker, S. H., Redfern, A. K., & Smith, D.L. (1992). A Snowball's Chance in Hell: Doing Fieldwork with Active Residential Burglars. *Journal of Research in Crime and Delinquency, 29* (May), 148-61

Yablonsky, L. (1962). *The Violent Gang*. New York: Macmillan.

Yu, E. Y. (1987). *Juvenile Delinquency in the Korean community of Los Angeles*. Los Angeles: Korea Times.

Yun, Y. (1977). Early history of Korean immigration to America. In H.C. Kim (Ed.), *The Korean Diaspora* (pp.33-46). Santa Barbara, CA: ABC-CLIO

Young, L. (1973). *The fractured family*. New York: McGraw-Hill

Zimring, F. E. (1981). Kids, groups and crime: some implications from a well-known secret. *Journal of Criminal Law and Criminology, 72*(3), 867-886.

Index